LEADERSHIP SKILLS FOR JEWISH EDUCATORS
A CASEBOOK

LEADERSHIP SKILLS

FOR

JEWISH EDUCATORS

A CASEBOOK

SHEILA ROSENBLUM

EDITOR

EDITORIAL BOARD

PREPARED UNDER A GRANT
FROM THE WEXNER FOUNDATION
TO GRATZ COLLEGE

BEHRMAN HOUSE, INC.
WEST ORANGE, NEW JERSEY

Designed by The Marketing & Design Group

Published by Behrman House, Inc.
235 Watchung Avenue
West Orange, NJ 07052

Library of Congress Cataloging-in-Publication Data

Leadership skills for Jewish educators: a casebook \ Sheila Rosenblum, editor.
    p. cm.
    ISBN 0-87441-555-1
    1. Jewish religious education–Case studies. 2. Jewish religious schools–
    Administration–Case studies. 3. Jewish educators–Case studies. 4. Educa-
    tional leadership–Case studies.
    I. Rosenblum, Sheila.
    BM103.L37 1994
    296.6'8–dc20   93-37122
                                                                         CIP

Manufactured in the United States of America

5 4 3 2 1

97 96 95 94 93

Table of Contents

Foreword

Since its inception as the first "Hebrew teacher's college" in the New World nearly a century ago, Gratz College has been in the forefront of innovation in the training of Jewish educators. While upholding the finest traditions and most deeply held values of our people, Gratz—today a much more broadly based institution of higher Judaic studies—has consistently sought to address the changing needs and challenges, techniques and technologies, required to transmit that heritage properly in a rapidly changing environment.

It was with this in mind that we at Gratz first proposed to develop an Executive Skills Program (ESP) within our Master of Arts in Jewish Education. For in addition to a rich Judaic background and sound pedagogical skills, those seeking a career as a senior administrator in the field of Jewish education need a whole range of competencies—from fund-raising and grantsmanship to computer literacy and personnel management—that were simply not part of such programs before. Indeed, in a conference held to plan for this project, virtually all the senior Jewish educators in attendance admitted to a total lack of formal training in these vital areas and to having relied on on-the-job training.

Concurring with our belief in the need for such a model program and with our plan for developing one was the Wexner Foundation of Columbus, Ohio, one of today's most creative and significant new funding sources in the fields of Jewish education and communal service. Its president, Rabbi Maurice Corson, and its director of institutional grants, Ferne Katleman, were most supportive throughout, awarding both an initial planning grant and then a far larger, two-year implementation grant. This funding enabled Gratz to develop two special team-taught courses in executive skills (one on managing human resources and one on managing material resources), to institute a major recruitment effort for the program, to cultivate a series of mentors to work with the executives-in-training, and finally to create the present casebook.

It is this casebook that, we feel, will have the broadest impact on the field, for it represents state-of-the-art knowledge and practice in Jewish educational administration. All the individuals involved in its preparation played key roles. Sheila Rosenblum, an educational consultant who conducted much of the field research via questionnaires and interviews that involved educators across the country, was also chiefly responsible for organizing and writing the book, and she did a superb job. Two members of the editorial board, Dr. Michael Austin, dean of the School of Social Work of the University of Pennsylvania, and Dr. Steven M. Brown, headmaster of the Solomon Schechter Day School of Philadelphia, brought their unique professional perspectives and experience to this challenging project. Finally, Dr. Diane A. King, associate professor of education at Gratz College and coordinator of the entire Wexner-funded project, did yeoman's service on the editorial board and as majordomo of a multifaceted, unprecedented project. Her devotion, professionalism, and good cheer throughout were appreciated by all.

As it approaches its centennial in 1995, Gratz College looks forward to its second century of service in the fields of Jewish education and Jewish studies.

Dr. Gary S. Schiff
President, Gratz College

Melrose Park, Pennsylvania

Preface

This volume, *Leadership Skills for Jewish Educators: A Casebook,* was prepared under the auspices of Gratz College of Melrose Park, Pennsylvania, with funding from the Wexner Foundation. It is designed to assist in the training of leaders in Jewish education and in the honing of the skills of those already in the field.

As it was conceived, the casebook was to have two parts, to correspond to the two parts of the Executive Skills Program at Gratz College: Managing Human Resources and Managing Material Resources. Based on reviews of the literature and on informal interviews with more than fifty educators, it became clear that dividing executive skills into these two parts is a useful heuristic device and a useful organizational mechanism for structuring a course sequence. In practice, however, the two domains overlap to a great extent. The management of human resources often entails the allocation of space, materials, and financial resources—all aspects of the management of material resources. Similarly, the management of material resources, which entails budget development and fund-raising, requires strong interpersonal management skills. And nowhere are the two domains interrelated more strongly than in a discussion of managing change.

We have learned much from the investigation and analysis of the field interviews, and what emerged is a casebook in two parts. Part One consists of an analysis of the case studies based on a framework for understanding the executive skills and behaviors of Jewish educators. The analysis and framework address issues relating to both human and material resources. Part Two consists of case vignettes that deal with both human resources and material resources. Many of the cases illustrate more than one management skill, including skills in the two overarching domains. Preceding the case studies themselves are Instructions for Using the Case Vignettes and a Table of Contents of Case Vignettes by Skill Areas.

The preparation of this volume was a team effort, and the author is indebted to the editorial board: Dr. Michael Austin, Dr. Steven M. Brown, and Dr. Diane A. King, for their ideas, suggestions, critiques, and support and for their contributions in measuring the materials against the needs and the reality base of the field. The author also acknowledges the support of the Wexner Foundation and of the Advisory Committee of the Wexner Executive Skills Project at Gratz College. Dr. King chaired the Advisory Committee, whose members included Dr. Marsha Bryan Edelman, Dr. Rela M. Geffen, Dr. Gary S. Schiff, Mr. Mervyn Tuckman, and Dr. Saul P. Wachs. Thanks are also expressed for the administrative and clerical assistance of Rochelle Cohen, executive secretary at Gratz College.

Most of all we are indebted to the many educators and executives who contributed their time and allowed the author to question them, often at length, about their experiences, both positive and negative, and about the many dilemmas they have faced at various junctures in their careers. They spoke with great candor and assisted us generously despite the valuable time these conversations took away from their primary task of leading and managing their educational programs. We are grateful for their participation and sincerely hope that this casebook will help them and others become more effective executives in Jewish education.

Sheila Rosenblum

Philadelphia, Pennsylvania

PART ONE
ANALYSIS OF CASE STUDIES OF JEWISH EDUCATORS

Chapter 1

▼

INTRODUCTION AND OVERVIEW

The research literature demonstrates that the sine qua non of effective schools is strong leadership, that an effective leader shapes the values, beliefs, structures, and practices of a school or educational community and is key to its success. The importance of leadership is also a theme in the literature on organizational excellence in both noneducational and educational settings; this literature often focuses on leadership that transforms people and organizations into improved and superior forms capable of the highest levels of accomplishment.

This book is about the skills Jewish educators need to lead and manage their organizations. To learn about these skills, you must first understand the way in which certain terms will be used in this book. Leadership and management are overlapping concepts, but they are qualitatively different. Leaders set the course for the organization; managers make sure the course is followed. Leaders make strategic plans; managers design operations to ensure that the plans are put into place. Leaders stimulate and inspire; managers use their influence and authority to translate the energy into productive work. Simply put, leadership is knowing what to do; management is knowing how to do it. When they need to be, good managers are also leaders; and leaders who cannot also manage may never see their dreams or plans translated into action. Both leadership skills and management skills are necessary in the management of human and material resources in the school setting.

These skills are particularly critical to the success of organizations whose primary mission is Jewish education, whether in a formal context or in an informal one. In many organizations one can expect there to be several individuals in management positions. But in Jewish educational settings this is often not the case. Because of the limited size and scope of most Jewish educational organizations, the administrative staff is often a single individual. Both management and leadership may devolve upon that person; he or she may be required to inspire plans as well as to execute them.

In the field of Jewish education, the stakes are high. The quality of the life of the Jewish community, if not the community's very growth and survival, may depend on good education. Because a community's support for Jewish education is voluntary, resources are generally limited, and other community interests often compete for them. Advocacy and support may be ambivalent, and the educational mission is often ambiguous. Thus, the executive skills required of Jewish educators may be even greater than those needed by other educators.

The Key Skills of Management and Leadership

The success of every manager and every leader depends on his or her skills in eleven key areas. The leadership and management skills that Jewish educators must possess, and that are the subject of this volume, include the following:

Defining vision and setting goals. The ability to define the vision of an organization and to set goals for it is a crucial characteristic of leadership. It is the mechanism by which leaders inspire, plan, create an organizational culture and ethos, and allow long-range goals to be transformed into the many large and small steps that make change happen. It is what sets apart the ordinary from the special.

Defining one's own role and the roles of others. The role of the Jewish educator may be ill defined, a factor that may have negative consequences for his or her professional effectiveness. Effective leadership is enhanced when the leader's role is well defined and the roles of others in the educational system, such as the members of the school board and other professionals in the organization, are clearly articulated as well. Skills associated with entering and terminating a position are especially important, because it is in these situations that defining the role may be particularly crucial.

Managing change. Organizations may function routinely and smoothly under skillful and careful management. But in order to respond to the needs of the school and the community and to changes in external conditions, and in order to avoid irrelevant education and the possibility of staff burnout, the executive must be able to manage the process of change. The change may be in the organization of the school, in the curriculum, in instructional strategies, or in a variety of other areas. Managing change is a skill that may differentiate the leader from the manager. Managing change requires vision, sensitivity to goals and mission, and knowledge of the factors associated with the process of change. It is also an area in which the necessity to integrate the management of human and material resources is especially evident.

Managing lay-professional relations. Jewish education takes place in organizational settings that are governed by voluntary boards and committees. Success at managing relations with the lay members of these boards and committees—by defining their roles, utilizing their skills, and gaining their support—can determine an executive's success.

Managing staff. Staff members are the backbone of an educational enterprise. Skills in hiring, firing, and supervising the staff and in facilitating their work are essential to the executive.

Relating to parents and students. Staying "close to the customer" is an important aspect of Jewish education. Parents and students are the executive educator's major constituencies, and dealing with them requires skills in both pedagogy and public relations.

Relating to other professionals in one's organization. The "other" professionals in an organization are those besides the teachers and staff members whom the executive supervises. Jewish educators are probably unique in the extent to which they must work with other professionals, such as those in the synagogue setting who are either directly or indirectly involved with the school. Since many Jewish educators work in a complex organizational environment, managing relationships in such an environment can be consuming if skills are not applied with care.

Managing day-to-day operations. Strong organizational and human relations skills are essential to the effective management of the day-to-day operations that consume the time of most administrators. Included among these skills are the abilities to deal with both competing priorities and the minutiae of running an organization. Without skills in this area, the organization would not function.

Managing oneself. Executives must be able to manage their own time and still meet their own needs. They may, for example, wish to continue their own studies or maintain contact with students, colleagues, and new ideas. The executive who manages his or her own time feels refreshed and vigorous.

Managing space. Managing material resources, such as space, is an important skill for the maintenance of an effective educational operation. It is especially important in settings where the school shares space with other groups, a not uncommon occurrence in Jewish education.

Managing funds. Without funds educational organizations cannot operate. Whether resources are scarce or ample, the acquisition and allocation of funds are critical executive skills.

Applying the Skills

Effectively carrying out the skills of management and leadership is the challenge all educational leaders face. Since many circumstances can influence the leadership process, knowing how and when to use these skills is crucial.

There is much we can learn about the leadership of educational organizations from the literature of organizational management, which emphasizes rationality, predictability, planning, and administration. These aspects of management undoubtedly apply in many successful, well-structured organizational settings, but it is notable that even in the last two decades management theorists have pointed out that most organizations, especially schools, do not resemble the rational, predictable, well-controlled settings that the textbooks tend to describe. Rather, they are much more likely to be influenced by political processes in the organization, by the politics of the environment, by the local culture, and by a variety of other factors, many of which defy predictability and order.

The Importance of Context and Environment

All these factors are highly applicable to the field of Jewish education. Jewish educators and their organizational settings are even more diverse and possibly more turbulent than those in the general community. For example, the general educational systems in the larger society are diverse in such areas as school level (the school may be elementary, secondary, or postsecondary), organizational type (the organization may be a school, a district office, a state or regional agency, a technical-assistance or resource agency), demographic setting (it may be urban, suburban, or rural), and size. But for the most part educational organizations in the general community are relatively standardized structures, and there are rather clear certification requirements and career paths for professional educators, including paths leading to administrative and executive positions.

Not so in Jewish educational settings. This became clear during a field-based effort to gather information about the experiences and dilemmas faced by professionals in the areas of formal and informal Jewish education. We conducted interviews with more than fifty educators in a variety of organizational settings in which Jewish education is the primary or secondary focus, including supplementary schools, day schools, central agencies in Jewish education, and Jewish communal agencies. The interviews, which were semistructured and anecdotal, focused on the background and experiences of the educators and on critical incidents they encountered in their dealings with staff, boards, parents, and other professionals, in their management of day-to-day operations and budgets, and in the myriad activities that constitute their jobs.

What we learned is that Jewish educators and the contexts in which they operate may be much more diverse than are general educators and the contexts in which they operate. Although the number of professional-training programs has increased in recent years, there is no defined and recognized career path for educational administrators, and the background and training of practicing administrators vary greatly. Some administrators were not formally trained as educators but entered the field because of a strong Judaic background. Others were trained as educators but not as administrators and were promoted to their position because of their willingness and availability. Still others had an educational and/or administrative background and were given the positions despite a weak background in Judaism and Jewish education; this is especially prevalent in areas where there is a dearth of qualified Jewish educators. Furthermore, whereas personal characteristics, such as approach to leadership and leadership style, may vary in similar ways for both general and Jewish educators, the factors of ideology and religious and cultural values may uniquely influence leadership and management behaviors among executives in the field of Jewish education.

We learned a great deal, too, about the real-life dilemmas and experiences of the educators we interviewed. In studying the content of the interviews, it became clear that a great many conditions exert strong influences on the leadership and management behaviors of Jewish educators. The three most important factors are the characteristics of the context in which the educator must function; the executive's personal background and experiences; and the guiding principles that suggest general norms for the use of executive skills and the choice of behaviors. These conditions and characteristics, as well as the relationships among them, are displayed in the figure on the following page. This figure depicts the conceptual framework guiding the analysis in this casebook.

Context

A first set of influences on leadership skills and behaviors relates to context. Educators must understand that there are significant contextual differences as they consider their leadership behaviors. The figure depicts the many important dimensions of context, but the most important contextual factor that influences the leadership skills an educator must possess is the type of organization in which he or she works.

Jewish educational administrators operate in several types of organizations. Although some skills apply to all these organizations, the diversity of organizations suggests that each may require the application of different approaches and skills by those in leadership roles.

Type of organization We have considered three types of organizations:

1. Formal schools (including supplementary schools and day schools), which have as their primary purpose the delivery of instruction to students. These schools require educational leadership skills and the ability to manage staff and the core technology of schooling, including curriculum, instruction, and interaction with parents.

2. Organizations that have as their primary purpose the delivery of a service (for example, training, technical assistance, or supervision) to schools. Such organizations include central agencies or bureaus of Jewish education. They require skills in dealing with interorganizational relationships and in working with administrators and teachers in client organizations.

INFLUENCES ON LEADERSHIP SKILLS

CONTEXT

TYPE OF ORGANIZATION

TYPE OF COMMUNITY

ROLE STRUCTURE

SIZE OF ORGANIZATION

STATUS OF ORGANIZATION

CONSUMERS

PERSONAL CHARACTERISTICS

TRAINING AND EXPERIENCE

IDEOLOGY

APPROACH TO LEADERSHIP

LEADERSHIP/MANAGEMENT SKILLS

SETTING VISION/GOALS

DEFINING ROLES

MANAGING CHANGE

MANAGING LAY/PROFESSIONAL RELATIONS

MANAGING STAFF

RELATING TO PARENTS AND STUDENTS

RELATING TO OTHER PROFESSIONALS IN ONE'S ORGANIZATION

MANAGING DAY TO DAY OPERATIONS

MANAGING SELF

MANAGING SPACE

MANAGING FUNDS

GUIDING PRINCIPLES

MISSION

PLANNING

ACCOUNTABILITY

REFLECTIVE PRACTICE

RESPECT

FLEXIBILITY

MAINTENANCE OF PROFESSIONAL DEMEANOR

CONCERNS ABOUT PHYSICAL ENVIRONMENT

FISCAL RESPONSIBILITY

VALUES

3. Organizations in which education is not the primary purpose but that have educational components within their structure or the strengthening of Jewish identity among their goals. This category includes Jewish community centers, Jewish camps, Jewish family-service agencies, and other communal agencies. These require persuasive skills in promoting educational foci as well as skills in managing one's own unique and perhaps ambiguous role in the organization.

The formal schools referred to above require additional clarification as a type of organization in which Jewish educators are operating. There is a wide array of formal schools, each with its own special conditions that have implications for the leader's role, degree of autonomy, and complexity of relationships (factors that will be described more fully in the following chapters). In the field of Jewish education, formal schools include several variants of the supplementary school.

The most common is the supplementary school that is typically organized and administered by a synagogue (and often called the congregational school); it operates after the secular school day and/or on weekend mornings. Other supplementary schools are the consolidated school (typically sponsored jointly by several synagogues) and the community school (typically operated as an independent organization, usually with support from the local federations of Jewish agencies).

Another type of formal school, and one that has a different set of professional challenges, is the day school, which offers both secular and Jewish studies. The day school may be unaffiliated with a particular denomination (that is, a community day school), it may be identified with a specific denomination and movement within Judaism, or it may even be linked to an individual synagogue.

Both supplementary schools and day schools conduct classes

in grades ranging from prekindergarten through high school. A type of formal school at the postsecondary level is the Hebrew college (though it may include a supplementary secondary school as well). Typically a nondenominational institution, the Hebrew college is found in several major cities and usually receives support from a federation.

The skills necessary for leading and managing these various kinds of formal schools are wide ranging and may need tailoring for the conditions specific to each.

Other contextual factors Other contextual factors may facilitate or constrain leadership. As depicted in the figure, they include the following:

1. Type of community. The setting may be urban or suburban, a small city or a large one, and the density of the Jewish population will vary from community to community. One example of this factor as a source of influence relates to the supply and demand of qualified personnel. In a small and relatively isolated community, the lack of a staff with a sufficient background and knowledge of Hebrew may affect the administrator's ability to implement a particular curriculum.

2. Role structure. In different organizations and different settings the administrative role may be part-time or full-time, or the position may be a combined role, such as educator-youth director or educator-cantor. The way in which the role is structured has implications for the scope and intensity of the administrator's activities, such as supervising staff, meeting with parents, and developing relationships with board members.

3. Size of the organization. Variations in size have many implications, not the least of which is the availability of such resources as money, space, and support systems within the

organization. Executives may need to adjust their practices and expectations to conform with the size constraints of the organization.

4. Status of the organization. The organization may be expanding, declining, or stable. It may also be undergoing major changes in the type of population it serves, in its ideology, or in its approach to ritual. Managing growth or decline can be very consuming and may deflect energy from other developmental activities.

5. Consumers. The values and attitudes of the parents and the supporters of the institution have a profound influence on the leadership processes. Communities may have traditions of educational excellence, or, conversely, they may have minimal expectations. The professional leader may choose to adapt to the status quo or undertake to change it.

Personal Background and Experiences

An administrator's personal characteristics also strongly influence the leadership and management processes. Certain personal characteristics help make administrators better leaders. For some these characteristics come naturally; for others they must be learned. Among the personal characteristics we have considered are the following:

1. Training and experience. Individuals with various amounts of training and experience find themselves in leadership and managerial positions. Some have spent many years in Jewish educational settings; others assume administrative positions with little or no training or experience. Some may need on-the-job training and may seek out opportunities for professional development.

2. Ideology. A Jewish educator's ideological approach (for example, his or her religious orientation or attitude toward Zionism) exerts a strong influence on the way he or she approaches the educational core of the executive's tasks. Sometimes that approach may come into conflict with the community's prevailing ideology. The educator may need to choose ways of reconciling the differences between his or her own approach and the community's expectations.

3. Approach. Managerial and leadership styles are subject to change, and each educator may come to the task with his or her own orientation. Some may take a technical-managerial approach to the job, concentrating on the day-to-day operations; others may favor a mentor-guide or facilitative approach, concentrating on supporting the professional development of the staff. Others may take a more directive approach. The approach that is used may or may not be the most appropriate for the particular situation.

The Guiding Principles of Leadership Practices

Whereas context and personal characteristics may have diverse influences on leadership and management processes, certain guiding principles are relevant to all executives as they use their leadership and management skills. Effective leaders apply these critical guiding principles to everything they do, thereby keeping their practices consistent and on an even keel in the face of changing circumstances and diverse pressures. Some of these principles are derived from well-established theories of leadership and organizational management. Others emerge from the value system that is part of the Jewish tradition. The following is a carefully selected list culled from the many guiding principles presented in the management literature; these principles have been chosen as particularly relevant for Jewish educators:

1. **Mission.** Effective organizations are driven by goals. These goals, and the standards by which they are measured, should be derived from the mission of the organization and should drive managerial practice. The principle of mission is especially effective when the executive has a strong and powerful vision of how the mission may be achieved.

2. **Planning.** Careful planning of all aspects of educational activity is essential for success. Planning is a crucial component of effective leadership and management practices.

3. **Accountability.** Executives should hold themselves and others accountable, linking desired behavioral ends to plans based on goals and standards.

4. **Reflective practice.** Reflective practice is a distinguishing feature of effective leaders and managers. Managerial practice should be guided by an analysis and understanding of both the dynamics of the organization and the personalities of the individuals.

5. **Respect.** Managerial practice and behaviors should clearly demonstrate respect for all in the educational system and its environment, including students, staff members, parents, other professionals, and lay leaders. This principle conforms with good managerial practice and good Jewish practice.

6. **Flexibility.** Flexibility is essential for effective educational and administrative practice. Standards and planning are important, but individuals and organizations are dynamic entities whose circumstances and needs are frequently unique. Not every activity or program can be carried out without modifications and adjustments.

7. **Maintenance of professional demeanor.** The executive should separate his or her professional and private lives, and not attend to private business or show personal biases while carrying out professional responsibilities.

8. **Concerns about the physical environment.** The quality of the environment contributes to the educational experience and can facilitate or hinder that experience. The environment need not be luxurious, but it must be conducive to learning, and it must demonstrate a respect for the staff and students and the importance of the Jewish educational experience.

9. **Fiscal responsibility.** The organization cannot function without responsible fiscal practices, including the continuous monitoring of budgets.

10. **Jewish values.** For Jewish educators adherence to Jewish values is the backbone of leadership and management. It is the distinguishing feature that influences their executive skills.

The Training of Jewish Educators

In sum, there is compelling evidence that the field is inordinately diverse, with educators operating in different contexts, coming to their positions with different backgrounds and different experiences, and offering different responses to a single set of guiding principles. Clearly the first skill that administrators or potential administrators must develop is the ability to assess and understand their position in this complexity; only then can they determine how to adapt to the system or try to modify it. In this process administrators must not ignore the political dimensions of the context or assume that the system is always rational.

The purpose of the volume is to assist in the training of leaders in Jewish education and in the honing of the skills of those already in the field; we mean to do this without duplicating the literature on leadership and management practices that is already available.

The remainder of Part One illustrates what we have learned about the framework for understanding the variety of influences on executive skills. We examine a set of leadership skills that all Jewish educators need. We show how educators must consider different conditions as they exercise their leadership skills. And we provide examples of how educators might adapt to the structure and the political environment in which they work.

We have selected a sample of leadership skills from the set of eleven that were presented earlier in order to present compelling evidence of the differences that administrators need to contend with in various circumstances. The sampled skill areas are managing lay-professional relations, managing staff, relating to other professionals in one's organization, managing change, and managing funds. These five areas are not more important than the other six, but they represent the diversity of skills in managing human and material resources.

The focus of Part Two is the case vignettes, which are meant as teaching aids. These vignettes are based on the actual experiences of educators in the field and are organized according to specific issues and topics. They are intended to exemplify the dilemmas administrators face and to help develop the problem-solving skills that are needed to address them. Each vignette is followed by questions that are meant to amplify thought and discussion about the issues raised in the vignette. Instructions for the use of the teaching vignettes by groups or individuals precede the cases themselves.

Chapter 2

▼

MANAGING LAY-PROFESSIONAL RELATIONS

Every nonprofit organization has a volunteer board, and thus it is not surprising that guidance on the relevant issues associated with lay-professional relations comes primarily from the literature on nonprofits. This literature assumes a regular ongoing board-executive relationship with regularized board procedures, a model that is pertinent in some ways to Jewish educational institutions, each of which has some sort of board that is a governing structure for the organization. Typically there is a governing board and a staff that is headed by an executive. In Jewish education the way in which this dyad operates varies widely, as does the authority structure, the composition of the board, and the nature of the relationship between the board and the executive, depending on the type of organizational setting. The following are examples of the relationships in different contexts and their implications for leadership skills.

Supplementary Schools

Supplementary schools, the most common Jewish educational institutions, exist in several forms. The type of lay board the educator must work with and the nature of the relationship between the professional and the board depend on whether the supplementary school is a congregational school, a consolidated school, or a community school.

The congregational school is, paradoxically, the simplest in structure but the most complex to administer. In part the complexity occurs because the school exists as a unit within a larger organizational structure—the synagogue. In this setting the educational leader is the school principal but not the chief executive in the organization in which the school is operating. In the typical congregational school setting there is a school board that sets policy and serves in an advisory capacity to the school. This board, the lay group that the educational leader deals with most directly, is frequently composed in part or totally of parents whose children currently attend the school. But there is also a congregational board of directors with which the administrator may have a working relationship, and there is the rabbi, who may be the organization's executive and who in many cases is considered the educator's supervisor. Thus, perhaps more than any other type of school, the congregational school presents the greatest challenges in establishing good lay-professional relations because the educator has multiple "bosses," and the relationship with each of them is often ambiguous.

Since it may serve multiple purposes in the synagogue, a congregational school is a politically complex environment. The fact that it may be parent driven is only one complexity. The principal may need to satisfy the professional staff, the board, and the membership in general while trying to run an educational enterprise based on sound educational principles. For these reasons skills necessary to conduct political (rather than purely rational) negotiations are especially critical in the congregational school.

Nonetheless, congregational schools, especially if they are neither large nor affluent, are likely to hire inexperienced administrators, who are unlikely to have acquired these key skills. And many Jewish educators begin their career in a school setting where the role, activity, and function of the board are not very well defined and their own roles are not well understood. Said one such administrator,

> When I came to the interview, they asked me a lot of questions about my experience, the amount of teaching I could do, and my willingness to work with a junior congregation. But when I asked them for a job description, they didn't have one in writing, and when we talked about it, it became a laundry list which different people on the committee contributed to. When I asked them whom I would be responsible to, they also looked confused and gave me different answers—like the school board, the president, the rabbi.

Procedures for decision making are frequently unclear, and as a result, the educator often makes decisions independently or in consultation with the school board chair, only to be confronted later by the board or by a newly appointed chairperson, as in this situation:

> I wanted to enroll in some courses in Judaica and in educational administration. I needed them for myself and also

to improve my capabilities as the principal. I informed my school committee chair that I would be taking the courses two mornings and one evening a week and asked her not to schedule any meetings on Wednesday nights during the semester. She agreed. I got a lot of flak from members of the board when they heard about it later.

The educational director must often contend with turnover among school board members. Even when there is a successful relationship, it is often only temporary. Parents who are on the school committee may serve for a limited number of years—when their children are in the school. When there is a strong board, the contribution of strong individuals may also be temporary, as the school committee is often a leadership training ground for the synagogue. The most successful members of the school committee are usually tapped for leadership roles in the congregation. A congregational school administrator described such an experience:

The first four years I had a really good working relationship with the school committee. The two chairs were really supportive, and we talked regularly. Then it seemed like within a very short time there was almost a total shift in the membership of the committee. There was a new temple president who appointed a chair without consulting me. The new chair was mainly interested in saving money and started giving me a real hard time.

It is not unusual for the school board to consist of two different types of people: those whose primary concerns relate to their own children and those whose primary concerns relate to the congregation in general—for example, they are interested in fiscal responsibility. A frequent complaint of school principals is the difficulty they face in trying to maintain or strengthen standards for the school. Their boards often reflect the short-term interests of the parent body and are not necessarily concerned with the quality and the intensity of the education. One principal explained,

> I am finding it really hard to hold the line on standards. We are one of the last holdouts on maintaining a standard of six hours a week for the religious school. One of those hours is already considered to be independent study. The board is trying to reduce it to be more in line with the neighboring synagogue schools. Parents on the board say it is just too hard to get the kids here on three different days. There are too many competing activities, and many of the mothers are working.

The executive's best relationship, his or her real working relationship, is typically with the chair of the school board. Working closely with only one individual, however, will not necessarily guarantee success. It is the challenge of the school executive to institutionalize the strengths of the school board as an entity and not to depend exclusively on the strengths and talents of a single individual. Nonetheless, this executive said,

> I talk to my chairperson almost every day. She is a real support to me and also buffers me from parents and from the board. If not for her, I really don't know how I would do my job. I can really talk to her about anything.

School board members and chairpersons are often women whose Jewish educational background is not strong but who are or have been educators in the public school system. Sometimes they have more education credentials than the school principal, who may have a strong background in Judaica and has taken on a part-time principalship on the basis of a little teaching experience or who may have become principal in combination with other roles, such as cantor, youth director, or assistant rabbi. In some cases the working relationship with the chairperson is a collaborative one, a situation that strengthens the principal's leadership capability, as in this situation:

> The chairperson is very knowledgeable about supervision skills, and her supervision of me has helped me be a better supervisor of the teachers. She helped me put accountability mechanisms in place that have changed what I look for in teachers and the kinds of teachers that we hire. She also taught me how important it is to set standards, such as requirements for bar mitzvah, and document them, because the standardization process is the great equalizer.

Lay-professional relations can be especially complex for the educational director of a congregational school who has multiple roles in the congregation. It is not unusual for him or her to serve also as the youth director, who is accountable to the youth commission, or as the cantor, who works with the ritual committee. The educational director may also be responsible for adult education and work with that committee as well. Although these additional lay groups may not have as much contractual authority as the school committees, the congregational professional has the additional responsibility of interacting with and satisfying several constituencies. One administrator described such an experience:

> I get along well with the school committee and the school committee chair. But I am also the official youth director,

since that is the way they were able to construct a full-time position for me. However, I really do not spend a lot of time on the youth program; the youth advisors take care of it. The youth commission chair and I do not get along.

Sometimes the multiple roles are viewed by the educational director as a strength in the job:

I think the fact that I am the youth director and work with the youth program has definitely strengthened my high school program. I love working with teenagers, and the youth and high school programs are very integrated. Before I came, there was a big dropout from the school after bar mitzvah. Now retention for the high school is very high.

Working well with the lay board may not be sufficient if the school board is not well positioned within the synagogue structure. The educator and the school board may be in agreement, but the school board may not wield sufficient influence at the synagogue board level to gain support for the school. Contending with this ambiguous authority requires political-negotiation skills that may be beyond the control of the educator, as in this case:

In my position as educational director, I help to develop the budget of the board of education and, with them I make a budget presentation to the budget committee of the board of trustees every year. These budget sessions are always frustrating. No sooner is one committee "educated" about the school's needs than the members change, and the whole process has to begin all over again. To complicate matters, the members of the budget committee have no connection with the religious school, and the board of education has no power base within the congregation. Finally, the school has a good reputation, and the program is going well. This leads budget committee members to believe that no funds for new programs are necessary—their response is "If it's not broken, don't fix it."

Consolidated Schools

A consolidated school is one that is sponsored by two or more congregations and typically was established because of those congregations' limited resources and enrollments. The school may serve elementary grades only, high school grades only, or both. A single executive runs the school, whose classes may meet in a single location or in multiple locations. All the participating congregations contribute to the finances and send their students to the school. The lay board of the school consists of representatives of the participating organizations. In some cases, a bureau of Jewish education is also represented, even though the school is linked to particular synagogues and not to the community at large.

Interviews with principals of consolidated schools reveal that the lay-professional relationship in those schools bears some similarities to that in the congregational school and enjoys some advantages lacking in the congregational school. Like the congregational school, the consolidated school is connected to other contexts—in this case the sponsoring congregations—but because it is not linked to a single context, it appears to take on some characteristics of a separate, if not independent, entity. Consequently, its board, even if it is composed of many parents, is more autonomous than the school committee in a typical congregational school and is not a body created by and responsible to a congregational board of directors. In fact, it appears that unlike their counterparts on a congregational school board, many of the board members of a consolidated school are more interested in the school itself rather than in protecting the interests of their synagogue or their own children. The principal, therefore, can spend less time on political issues and has less of a need for board members or the chair to serve as a buffer between him or her and parental or membership pressures. If the board is active, many of the issues it deals with are educational. The educator is less likely to need to deal directly with the synagogues' boards of directors. Said one director of a consolidated school,

> When I started working with the school board from the combined school, I was at first concerned about the turf issues of each congregation. But I found that this community had a strong tradition of lay involvement, and the best way to get the help that I needed and to use their talents was to create a set of working subcommittees. We created four groups to work on curriculum, personnel, school evaluation, and finance. People became more task oriented than turf oriented, and they became fully invested in that aspect of the school. Some members of the working committees were not on the full school board, but the chairs worked with me and reported to the board. Sometimes I worked hand in hand with the committee, such as the time we created a course of study or worked on the evaluation plan.

The school's relative isolation from the sponsoring congregations sometimes increases the principal's autonomy. Board members who serve as representatives of their congregation may be less concerned with issues because their organization does not "own" the school. One principal remarked,

They are very satisfied with what I do and are glad not to have to worry about the high school. They are supportive and make suggestions, but mostly they are happy to leave the running of the school to me.

The consolidated school's relative independence has negative aspects as well as. No one organization owns the school, but the school does not necessarily have fiscal autonomy. And the greater the number of participating organizations, the harder it is for board members to muster leadership, commitment, and involvement of parent groups or their own boards—unless there is strong dissatisfaction with the school.

Day Schools

Lay-professional relations in a day school share certain characteristics with those in communal agencies, in that both organizations have a governing board and a full-time executive. Although linked to a somewhat larger context than the congregational school or the consolidated school—a federation as a funding source or the relevant denominational movement as a philosophical basis—the day school is probably the most independent school in Jewish education in terms of its lay-professional relations. Here the executive works directly with the board on policy issues. The schools are more independent than are communal agencies, since they raise most of their own funds through tuition, direct fundraising, or negotiations with the federations.

Day school leadership differs significantly from that of a supplementary school. Although the division of responsibility between the executive and the board is not always clear, particularly in the area of setting policy, there is more clarity about the educational role of the professional, and the professional does not have to contend with other "bosses," such as a synagogue president or a rabbi. (The exception is the day school that is formally attached to a single congregation, a setup that is seen occasionally.) The director is clearly the executive, the educational leader, and the school manager. As in a supplementary school, however, the board's natural constituency is the parent body, and often a large proportion of the school's lay leaders are parents. Therefore, it is important that the executive have the political skills to mediate between the interests of the school and those of the individual parents. Said one day school principal,

> There are some parents or former parents who are powerful on the board and who think they can run the school. They have opinions about teachers based on their kids' preferences. They make demands or statements that they would never do in a public school or even in another kind of private school.

The feeling among the day school directors we interviewed is that they enjoy a more professional relationship with their lay boards than do the directors of most supplementary schools. But it is the challenge of the day school director to professionalize the relationship even further.

Other Organizations and Agencies

The leadership skills needed to manage the relations with lay groups in Hebrew colleges, central agencies, or Jewish communal agencies are equally important but differ from those needed in the schools described above because their boards do not have a natural constituency, such as parents. Board members are more likely to be community leaders, only some of whom have a particular interest in the goals of the agency. They may join the board for a variety of reasons—for example, to gain status, to network socially, or to make business contacts—but they may also be power brokers in the community who are able to influence the growth and survival of both the agency and the executive.

A benefit of working with this type of board is that the lay leaders may be objective, since they are not primarily concerned with the Jewish education of their own children. But because the board members have no personal stake in the organization, the executive must nurture them carefully in order to maintain their support and interest in the organization.

These "other" organizations and their professional leaders are dependent on their boards for funding, legitimation, and approval. The professionals are accountable to their boards, but in order to get their vision approved and implemented, they must expend significant energy "educating" the board members. The executive faces the challenge of gaining the support of the board. To achieve this support, the executive must educate the board about the ideology of the organization and foster the board's commitment. One executive successfully met this challenge:

> I saw bright people on the board, people who cared enough to be involved. But I invested an inordinate amount of energy reasoning with them every step of the way because they would become increasingly involved if they felt that any of the ideas emerged from them. I plant the seeds, then they initiate. Why is this important? I get paid, they don't. If they can get a sense of achievement, nachas, why shouldn't they? Indeed, the success is dependent on them—fund-raising, authority. I need their good will. I ask, Why should they do this unless they get a sense of accomplishment?

Sometimes, as in the following example, the extreme nurturing of the board may reduce staff morale:

A staff member had the idea of mounting an important educational and cultural event—a biblical archaeology exhibit and lecture series. I presented it to the board and got strong interest from two board members whom I have been trying to "develop." They like archaeology and became supporters of the event. They agreed to co-chair the committee planning the event. The staff person who did the work complained to me bitterly that he thought that I gave all the credit and recognition to the lay people.

Conclusion

The focus of this section has been the challenges executives face as they try to manage the lay-professional relationship. A good working relationship with the lay board enhances the potential for effective leadership no matter what the setting, but, as we have seen, the difficulties to be surmounted are various and complex. Nonetheless, we can derive from the examples presented here several general dimensions of the relationship:

1. defining and clarifying the respective roles of the executive and the board
2. developing a shared understanding of accountability mechanisms and the authority structure
3. establishing regular channels of communication
4. establishing procedures that facilitate the smooth transition and succession of lay leadership

The case vignettes in Part Two illustrate these dimensions.

Chapter 3

▼

MANAGING STAFF

Professional educational adminis-
trators must manage internal and external relations effectively.
But perhaps the most essential educational leadership skill for
such administrators is the ability to work effectively with their
staff. Too often the political exigencies of dealing with board
members, parents, and funding agencies distract administrators
from their primary goal of exercising educational leadership. No
matter what the setting, facilitating the staff's work is the key
ingredient of effective leadership. As one veteran educator stated,

Faculty are the most important part of the school, and it is
important to laboriously develop one-on-one contact and
relationships. It was always the hardest but most critical

part of my job. Board members are enablers; parents are supporters. But the acid test for the school is the educator, and we are totally dependent on the educator to make the endeavor work.

This chapter presents some of the variables, both contextual and personal, that influence a leader's interaction with his or her staff. Interviews with professionals in formal and informal Jewish educational settings confirmed that there are three key elements to the process of managing staff: hiring and firing, providing supervision, and facilitating work. These elements are strongly affected by the background and experience of the executives and by the way they define their role. But the capacity to manage staff is equally influenced by the type of organization in which the administrator is working and other factors relating to context, such as the structure of the administrator's role, the organizational structure of the school, and the availability of financial resources. The dilemmas administrators face in regard to staff relations in various contexts are described below.

Supplementary Schools

The management of staff in a supplementary school is hampered by several factors involving the capacities and commitments of both the administrators and the teachers. Many administrators are employed part-time or have multiple roles in the organization, only one of which is educational administration. Thus, an administrator may be able to commit only a limited amount of time and energy to this role. But even if the administrator is a full-time educational director, the school itself operates on a limited schedule, and the teachers work part-time. For many, teaching in a religious school is a second job; it is rare that teaching in a supplementary school is an individual's primary career.

Whether the teachers are committed to teaching as a career or not, the time limitations on their involvement with the school put severe constraints on the administrator-teacher relationship. Teachers' salaries are low, and there is a limit to the number of out-of-class hours administrators feel they can demand of their teachers. Typically they require attendance at some staff meetings, and in some settings there are contractual in-service demands—usually made by the central agency. But the hours for in-class observation and supervision are few. All classes in the school may meet during the same four or five hours a week. Teachers with experience are likely to get little or no direct supervision. One supplementary school administrator explained,

> During the time that classes are in session, everything is happening. I am constantly either solving crises with kids or teachers, putting out brushfires, rushing to staff a class for a teacher who was delayed, and so on. The phone keeps ringing, or parents insist on talking to me—since they are driving carpool and decide to hang around anyway. Everything is truncated in those few hours, and it is hard to control. I know I should be out in the classes more, observing teachers, providing support, but it is sometimes very difficult to get out of the office.

The irony is that many teachers in supplementary schools have the greatest need for supervision and assistance because they are inexperienced or lack professional training. They may be well intentioned, committed, sincere, and have a strong Judaic background but lack strong instructional skills. In small cities or isolated areas the reverse may be true. It is often difficult in such areas to find teachers who have the necessary strong Judaic background, even if they have the requisite teaching skills. In both situations the need for supervision and support, both substantive and peda-gogic, is great.

Many teachers feel uncomfortable or insecure about having an administrator observe them in their classroom. This applies to vet-eran as well as novice teachers. It is especially true of veteran teachers who have not been supervised recently or who feel self-conscious about having new, young administrators evaluate them. It is a challenge for the administrator to apply diplomacy as well as supervisory skills in interacting with these teachers. One young administrator said,

> One older teacher told me that she didn't think there was anything I could tell her about teaching that she didn't already know, and I agreed. But I told her that I would like to be like an extra pair of eyes, sort of a video camera in her room. She liked that idea. I was careful to praise her and let her know that she taught a really inspired lesson. But I also pointed out things that she may not have noticed. As time went on, she kept telling me that she became a much more "aware" teacher, having been observed formally.

Many educational directors in supplementary schools have limited supervisory training or experience. There is no well defined career ladder for educational administrators in supplemen-tary schools, and if one wants a professional career in Jewish edu-cation, one can advance to a leadership position in a supplemen-tary school at a young age.

Thus, young educators with limited experience are sometimes thrust into a position where they are supervising teachers who are older and more experienced than they. In small or relatively isolat-ed communities they also may be supervising staff members who are related to other staff members in the congregation or who are themselves members of the congregation. Supervising these teachers can put undue political strains on the administrator, who must skillfully balance professional responsibility with the potential hostility of influential members of the congregation:

> One of the hardest times that I had as a supervisor was when I had to deal with a teacher who was also the daughter of the president of the congregation. She was having serious personal problems in her life, but she was taking it out on the kids. I just couldn't get her to realize that or to try to separate her personal life from her teaching. A lot of parents complained about her behavior in the classroom, and I finally had to let her go in the middle of the year. Lots of important people never forgave me for that, and my position got very uncomfortable.

Perhaps as a result of inexperience, many administrators in supplementary schools find that managing the administrative details of the school—including scheduling and dealing with buses, vendors, and supplies—consumes much of their time. The remainder of their school day can be consumed by interactions with parents and other staff members in the organization. Thus, they avoid supervising the teachers directly, although they may rationalize this behavior in many ways. One administrator said,

> I tend to hire people who I feel are competent and who know what they are doing. I will provide curriculum materials but give them a lot of leeway to teach in the way that they want. I don't like to crowd them; after all, they are professionals. But one teacher was very angry because she wanted some benefits from the synagogue—including free

membership, which they would not provide. She took it out on me. But when we talked, she admitted that what she really wanted was more guidance and support from me. She felt very isolated. I know I need to make more time to spend with the teachers and to visit the classrooms. I guess I am not as comfortable in that role as I would like to admit, and I have to learn to do it better.

The quality of education in a supplementary school is greatly enhanced when the principal develops good supervisory and support skills. Principals need to explore ways to develop methods of supervision that maximize their capabilities and meet the needs of their staff. One educator described his method:

I do not use a formal observation form with an explicit set of criteria because I do not want to tie them or myself to the categories. However, I do have a set of factors that I consider when I observe a teacher. These include content, the logic of the content, age appropriateness, variety of strategies, classroom management and control, and the level of interaction in the class.

Some administrators find ways to bring out the best in their teachers and to facilitate their teaching skills:

I try to get them to like what they are teaching and to teach what they like, and I try to make it possible for teachers to help each other. This was made possible by a structural change in my school a few years ago. We stopped scheduling classes for each grade on alternative days. For example, because of scheduling nightmares, we no longer gave a choice of Monday and Wednesday or

Tuesday and Thursday for the midweek *gimel* class. All multiple sections of the same grade level would meet at the same time. This meant that teachers were teaching the same grade at the same time, and if they wanted to, they could team-teach and even trade subjects. It also helped me pair new or inexperienced teachers with veteran teachers. Then I just let it happen.

Day Schools

The day school is a more formal educational setting than many supplementary schools in that both teachers and administrators view themselves primarily as professional educators. Staff positions are full-time, and even those teachers who take on second jobs typically define their day school job as the primary one. Some day schools are unionized, and in such cases the teachers' roles are well defined, as are the evaluation procedures.

The day school setting is much more conducive to a traditional supervisory relationship between administrator and staff than is the supplementary school setting. Despite all the duties a day school principal must carry out, most administrators view educational leadership as a major part of their role. This includes working with teachers on a regular basis, providing opportunities for teachers to work collegially, and enabling teachers to get the help they need.

There are problems with staff relations in the day school, nonetheless. A common source of unrest is the difficulty inherent in managing the dual curriculum of general and Judaic studies. Integrating the two faculties is often one of the biggest leadership challenges. The day school administrator may feel inadequate in one or the other discipline and may need to structure the supervisory process innovatively. The administrator is also more likely to relate best to the staff in his or her own discipline, as in this situation:

> When I came to the school, staff morale was very low. I had to put a lot of energy into creating a relationship with the staff, especially since part of my vision for the school involved more intensive staff development. I spent a lot of time drinking coffee in the teachers' lounge. Naturally, I gravitated toward the Judaic studies teachers because that is my field, and I identify with them. But the other teachers came to really resent that.

As is the case in supplementary schools, not all principals of day schools have been trained as supervisors. Each school may set the standard for the credentials it seeks in an administrator, such as advanced degrees in Judaic studies or education, but it does not necessarily require administrative credentials. Standards and credentials for the teachers, especially teachers of Judaic studies, vary even more. Thus, day school administrators need strong supervisory skills. The administrator is often deflected from fulfilling the role of educational leader by competing responsibilities, including dealing with parents, nurturing board members, raising funds, and recruiting students. Many day schools are either too small or too strapped financially to afford additional administrative staff. Even when such staff is available, many principals are not skilled at delegating tasks. Choosing to work with the teaching staff sometimes means neglecting other responsibilities:

> I get a lot of calls and interruptions from parents, some of whom are also board members. I have been told by the consultant that it is important for me to work on "board development," respond to calls, visit hospitalized board

members—things like that—and to solidify relationships in the community. But I would rather be teaching a class or giving a lesson to teachers. I see myself primarily as a teacher.

There are several career paths on the route to day school director, some of which lay good groundwork for relating to teachers. Some administrators get experience as principals of supplementary schools. Others may move from teacher to master teacher to administrator of the day school. In the latter case a strong identification with teachers may help in developing supervisory skills. One new director explained,

I am just learning to supervise, so I take copious notes when I observe teachers. Sometimes I disagree with what the teacher is doing, but I try to maintain the teacher's perspective. I also give them a choice regarding the scheduling of the observation. The teacher may choose to have me come in for one formal lesson or to have me come in and out for one week. I am close enough to it so that I know what the teachers' problems are, and I also know what kind of assistance I valued as a teacher. But you do have a broadened view when you are working as the administrator. My past experiences in different kinds of schools do help.

Other Organizations and Agencies

The leadership skills needed to manage the staff of a central or communal agency are equally important, but they are different from those needed in schools. In schools of all types, teachers may be supervised and supported, but in the last analysis they work independently in their classrooms. Even though schools may be hierarchical, the teacher is largely autonomous, and much of the work is conducted behind closed doors. This type of structure, together with the time constraints discussed above, influences the administrator-teacher relationship.

In community agencies, however, the situation is somewhat different. Although staff members have independent functions and projects, the potential for team building and collaborative work is greater than it is in schools, and opportunities to supervise or influence the staff may be greater. Nonetheless, a challenge lies in the position of the educational leader within the agency. In communal agencies such as federations or Jewish community centers, the person responsible for promoting educational ventures is not likely to be the chief executive. Thus, in order to influence staff and facilitate an educational program or focus, it may be necessary to "manage up" as well as laterally and down. This situation may generate conflicts for the educator, as in this case:

> It is really a strain to do this job when the education person is not the CEO. The CEO is the gatekeeper and will often not let me use my expertise or promote my project. He picks projects for political reasons—or to satisfy the big fund-raisers. But I have to work around him as well as through him in order to do what I think is important Jewishly and educationally.

Conclusion

This chapter has focused on the challenges facing educational leaders as they try to supervise and support their staff. Helping a staff to increase its effectiveness may be the essence of good leadership. But as we have seen, administrators find this challenge very difficult in many settings. In addition, many administrators have less than adequate preparation for the role.

Several principles of staff support and supervision become apparent from examining the evidence presented in this chapter:

1. Despite administrative difficulties and competing demands on their time, administrators must make the support and supervision of their staff a major priority.
2. Given the constraints of time and resources, administrators must seek innovative ways to provide or facilitate support for their staff.
3. Administrators can positively affect staff morale and efficacy by encouraging teachers to be involved in areas they like or in activities they feel they can do well.

Several vignettes presesented in Part Two further amplify the issues of staff relations.

Chapter 4

▼

RELATING TO OTHER PROFESSIONALS IN ONE'S ORGANIZATION

A unique feature of Jewish educational administration is that in many organizational settings the administrator operates as neither the chief executive officer nor the only executive officer. While Jewish educational administrators share with administrators in other settings the need for executive skills in managing staff and external relations, they spend a great deal of time interacting with other professionals in the organization. The relationships that develop from these interactions may become complicated if the priorities of the other professionals differ considerably from those of the educator.

In this chapter we describe some of the situations administrators find themselves in and some issues they must face in relating to other professionals. We also present the leadership skills that the educator must use in order to manage effectively relations with other staff members in the organization.

Supplementary Schools

Supplementary schools are the most common Jewish educational institutions, and they present the executive with the most complex environment. As described in Chapter 2, the school executive must deal with a school board and a synagogue board. But this educator must also interact with several other professionals in the organization—for example, one or more rabbis, a cantor, an executive director, a ritual director or sexton, a youth director, a nursery school director, and support staff. Some of these professionals may be peers in the organizational structure; others may exert authority over the school and the executive.

The rabbi may play a strong role in the school, and such a situation can be delicate for the school principal. One supplementary-school principal reported,

> My rabbi teaches the confirmation class and also participates in the curriculum committee. We recently revised the religious school curriculum, and I sometimes had to juggle my interests and perspectives with his. I guess he is the boss and I only work here part-time, but sometimes it is confusing as to who is the principal here.

Sometimes the rabbi plays less of a leadership role in the school:

> When I first came to this school ten years ago, the rabbi expressed a strong interest in the school, and I reported to him regularly. Gradually I came to realize that he rarely

made any suggestions or requests, and I began to meet with him less frequently. Maybe he was satisfied with the way things were going, and as long as there were no major complaints, he didn't need to pay much attention. I invite him to some meetings and events and he comes occasionally. Sometimes I feel he should actually make his presence felt with the students and staff more than he does.

At other times there may be potential conflict between the rabbi and the principal:

Part of my job is to run the junior congregation services. Sometimes, especially on the holidays, many parents prefer to attend our services with their children rather than attend the main services in the sanctuary. I don't think the rabbi is too pleased about this, but it is not my fault if the parents know us better than they know him and want to be in our service.

But interacting with the rabbi can also be a positive and supportive experience, as this administrator explained:

I have a wonderful working relationship with the rabbi. He is both knowledgeable and interested in the school, but he respects my position and my professionalism. He has been enormously supportive of school interests with the board and has helped me a lot with parents, students, and with ideas. I don't think I could run this school as well without his involvement.

Often the stress of dealing with the other professionals in the synagogue is greater if the line of authority is unclear. Frequently, for example, the cantor teaches music in the school and gives bar and bat mitzvah instruction, yet it isn't always clear whether the cantor is operating as an autonomous professional in the organization or as a member of the school staff who is thus supervised by the educational director. Because of the visibility of the cantor's skill at instructing the bar and bat mitzvah students, as well as the discrete nature of the instruction, the cantor may be strong-willed about his or her role. The relationship between cantor and educational administrator may be successful, or it may require delicate negotiation.

Similarly, the director of a congregational school must establish a good working relationship with the executive director of the synagogue, who often has major control over the allocation of such resources as space and support staff time. The school director may be competing for resources with the youth program and the nursery school, and this competition may hinder the kind of collaborative kinship among the professional staff that is important to effective programming.

At best these relationships require a delicate balance, which the educational director is not always able to control. Sometimes the balance is facilitated by the rabbi or the executive director through regular staff meetings. But often the organization provides few formal structures by which to promote good relationships, and it is up to the individual administrator to maintain harmony and, at the same time, promote the best interests of the school.

Consolidated Schools

The relationships among professionals in a consolidated school are even more ambiguous than those among professionals in a congregational school. Although directors of a consolidated school must relate to the rabbis of several congregations, they may have more autonomy than directors of a congregational school because they depend less on any one organization. In addition, some of the issues regarding relations with cantors will be simplified if the individual congregations, rather than the consolidated school, are responsible for bar and bat mitzvah instruction, for then contact with the cantors may be limited.

Often the relationship with the local building administrator is of most concern. Typically the consolidated school is housed in the building of one of its constituent schools or in another agency. The director must relate to the building's administrative staff, and the relationship may be tenuous, as in this case:

When I was principal of the community high school, we met in one of the synagogues. But we were like the proverbial stepchild that got everything last or had to gently ask for all favors. Since we were not "owned" by the host congregation, the executive director and staff did not feel responsible to us and regarded the synagogue needs as the first priority. I had to very carefully work through the host rabbi and school director when I had problems or needs, and it wasn't always comfortable.

Day Schools

Directors of day schools must manage relations with their staff and other administrators in the school. But unless the school is housed in a synagogue and is part of a synagogue structure, the director is the only chief executive officer in the building.

When the day school is housed in the building of another organization, such as a synagogue or an agency, the director must manage relations with the administrator of the building and may encounter problems similar to those encountered by directors of supplementary and consolidated schools.

Day school directors are in charge of most of the school's internal functions. In larger schools there may be a financial manager or a business manager, and this person may report to the board rather than to the principal. In that case there is potential for strain in the relationship between the director and other administrative personnel.

Day school directors do have to manage relations with external organizations, such as synagogues and federations. They must work with rabbis to recruit students and win lay support and with the federation and other agencies to solicit financial support. As educational leaders they must also work with both secular and Jewish agencies providing technical assistance and resources. They may work with central agencies and bureaus to enhance staff development, to set up special programs, and to make use of resource centers. They may also work with regional agencies that provide support for special education and supplement the school's general education program. In addition, they have to obtain or maintain state certification, meet state-mandated standards, and work with accreditation agencies and myriad other external agencies. All these interactions require interpersonal and interorganizational skills, as well knowing where and how to obtain resources, and they all add significantly to the complexity of the day school director's job.

Other Organizations and Agencies

Jewish educators in communal agencies whose primary mission is not education face a different challenge in managing relations with other professionals. For example, the director of the Jewish Family Life Education program in a Jewish family service agency faces the challenge of "educating" others in the agency about the importance of JFLE and its need for time and resources.

When the educator is also the agency's director, managing relations with others in the agency requires skills in vision, setting goals, and supervising. One director said,

> I constantly reinforce the mission of the agency and its Jewish-ness whenever I hire and supervise staff and in the programming that I develop.

The educator who is not the agency's director must be skilled in persuading peers as well as supervisors and in guarding the agency's educational mission. These skills may also be required in community settings, such as Jewish community centers and summer camps. The lack of support for the mission may be frustrating and isolating, and the educator may need to seek support by networking outside the organization.

A different challenge exists for administrators and staff members of central agencies and bureaus of Jewish education. In such agencies staff members interact with other professionals in the organization as individuals or as members of a team. Each staff member may have a different role or a different area of responsibility. The challenge arises in the way staff members relate to professionals when they provide services—for example, in synagogue schools or day schools. The way in which they gain entry and legitimize their services depends on yet another set of executive skills, those involved in regulating organizational boundaries.

Conclusion

This chapter has focused on managing relations with other professionals in the organization in which the executive's school is operating. The conditions affecting these relations vary according

to the type of organizational setting, but in no case is the executive isolated from other professionals, and his or her ability to work effectively with others can certainly enhance the successful operation of the educational enterprise.

Our field interviews reveal several dimensions of the relationship between the executive and other professionals; these can serve as a guide to successful relations:

1. Maintain the standards and interests of the school or the program, but at the same time remain flexible and understanding.
2. Keep lines of communication open.
3. Help define and clarify the respective roles, responsibilities, and lines of authority of each of the professionals in the organization.
4. Maintain respect and understanding of the roles and responsibilities of others.

Case vignettes presented in Part Two provide opportunities for further amplification and discussion of these issues.

Chapter 5

▼

MANAGING
CHANGE

All executives must face the challenge of managing change in their organizations. More so than any other executive skill, effectively managing change requires a successful blend of management and leadership, for it is the leader who sets the course for the organization, orchestrates the strategic planning, develops and shares a vision, and stimulates, inspires, and influences those who will help carry out the change. Although leadership may be essential for successful change, it is not sufficient. The management skills necessary for carrying out the operational plans, for translating the energy into productive work, and for turning visions into workable agendas and seeing that they happen are also key to the change process.

For Jewish educators the distinction between leadership and management is a vexing one because in most settings the executive must lead the organization as well as maintain it. There is little room for differentiating those functions. The educational leader must act on a continuum of demands, simultaneously understanding and coping with ordinary problems and daily routines, making situational adjustments, and dealing with the challenges of change. Too easily the leader can effect change carelessly and respond to changing needs without adequate care.

Managing change is also the arena in which the distinctions between managing human resources and managing material resources are the most blurred. It is difficult to envision a situation in which an executive could mount a major curriculum revision without engaging and supervising the staff on the one hand and considering the cost on the other. Similarly, the need to manage a school's growth or decline must entail considerations of staffing, class size, the use of space, and the need for budget increases or cuts. The literature on managing change is replete with discussions of who participates in the planning, the decision-making process, the process of adopting new ideas and programs, and the empowerment of the staff in the adoption and implementation processes. It also contains many discussions of the human and material factors that affect the implementation of change and the role external resources—both technical assistance and material resources—play in the process.

For Jewish educators the complexities of managing change are complicated further by the nature of the organizational context and the experience and skills of the staff. In this chapter we will discuss the experience of managing change in different contexts and its implications for the skills involved in leadership.

Supplementary Schools

Of all the settings in Jewish education, that of the supplementary school has faced the most criticism and the greatest call for change. The schools are variously seen as requiring too many hours or too few, as being unchallenging or too demanding, unruly or overly strict, unimaginative, superficial, and frivolous.

For a variety of reasons executives in supplementary schools face the greatest challenges in managing change. First, many complain that they do not have a clear mandate and are subject to the conflicting demands of parents, the school board, and other professionals in the organization, as in this case:

> I am committed to providing as good a Jewish education as possible in this school. I am trying to improve the standards, expand the curriculum, enforce requirements for attendance, encourage a greater knowledge of and love for the *Tanach*. We've even had winners in the city's *Chidon Tanach*. But I am being challenged by a movement of parents who want to reduce the Hebrew school to two days a week, and the rabbi is worried about alienating some of these important families.

Like this executive, many directors of supplementary schools feel they do not have a sufficient power base from which to manage the process of change. Their schools are not systems unto themselves but part of a larger system over which they have little control.

Others feel they do have the power, and they even envision what they want to accomplish for the school, but they do not necessarily envision a way to manage the process successfully. Too many executives set about leading the process of change unilaterally.

This method can effect change, but it does not necessarily ensure the commitment of those who must make the change work. Such was the experience of one educational director:

> When I first came to this school, things were working well. There was a cadre of experienced teachers, and they knew what they were doing. But I came to realize that there was no coherence to the school; there was no theme, vision, or sequential curriculum. With the consent of the school board and the agreement of the rabbi, I spent the summer writing a mission statement for the school and a four-year curriculum. Before school opened in the fall, I did an in-service for the staff. But it is taking a while for them to get used to the changes, and I am not sure they are all implementing them successfully.

What this principal lacked is an understanding that people are likely to resist change, especially if they have not participated in the change process. It is not enough to have a vision of how the organization should be operating; one must also know how to get there. It is the rare visionary in a supplementary school who has the capacity to mobilize people and resources in order to achieve change.

Directors of supplementary schools are typically generalists and unlikely to have an administrative staff to assist them. They have many responsibilities—completing administrative paperwork, hiring staff, scheduling, dealing with parents, special programs, and transportation. Some directors work part-time and may have other jobs. Many work in fairly isolated communities and do not have colleagues nearby or opportunities to communicate with others in the region. Thus, many do not have the luxury or the resources to develop ideas that can help improve their schools.

Nonetheless, a positive development in the field of Jewish education has been the increased capacity of educators to be users of knowledge—to acquire and use new ideas and programs that have been developed elsewhere. This capacity has been enhanced by changes in the ways in which many bureaus of Jewish education and central agencies are now operating and by the growth of organizations like CAJE (Coalition for the Advancement of Jewish Education) and the mini-CAJE conferences around the country. As one part-time principal said,

> I was coasting along in my school. Not much new was happening. It was at best a maintenance operation or worse. When there were problems, I felt frustrated about my ability to make changes, and there were no real mentors around me. I heard about CAJE, and my school board agreed to subsidize my participation in the conference. I picked up materials, got new ideas, and networked with people whom I now keep in touch with. I feel much more confident in passing materials on to my teachers and encouraging them to try innovations in their classrooms. I am now beginning a new effort in family education. I feel much more confident in myself and in my ability to make changes happen.

Despite such efforts, changes are typically small in scale or programmatic in nature. Although not unheard of, it is the rare supplementary school that has undertaken or considered a more intensive strategic planning process.

Day Schools

Unlike supplementary schools, day schools are typically independent systems; only occasionally are they linked organically to a host organization. Thus, the day school executive has more control over managing change, subject, of course, to financial constraints and the governance of the board of directors. If the school receives a subsidy from a federation of Jewish agencies, the federation may also impose constraints on the school's operations.

Managing change in a day school varies according to the organization's stage in its life cycle. When a school is new and growing, the executive faces the challenges of adding staff, adding grade levels, and working with the staff, the board, and the parent groups to develop the school's philosophy and mission. Once the school has reached a state of equilibrium, changes may involve negotiating among competing priorities, as in this situation:

> We spent hours deciding when it would be best to start the teaching of Bible, whether we should do more integration of the general and Jewish studies, how to give equal "prime time" to both departments. Up until recent times we made many of these decisions by consensus. But now we are getting larger, and we are losing the ability to make decisions that way. There are more special interest groups within our midst.

Day school directors also work with a professional teaching staff, whose members may have strong ideas and commitments of their own. Like their counterparts in public schools, teachers in day schools may resist change or interference in what they consider to be their areas of professional autonomy. Although the thoughtful and skilled leader may have a holistic picture of the school that the classroom teacher does not share, it takes strong skills involving human relations to bring the school community together to share that vision and to facilitate the adoption of that vision by others.

Making change happen in a day school can be facilitated by the accreditation process that most day schools must undertake. While some directors and their boards may have the foresight to put a strategic planning process in place on their own, the self-study process required for accreditation can also result in some far reaching changes. One day school director described the process:

> The team effort for the self-study in this school had a profound influence on the operations and the changes in the way that teachers relate to each other and the school as a whole. People now realize how disjointed some of our programs were and how useful it would be to do joint planning. I now also have a clearer understanding of what teachers expect of me as a leader and what they feel would be most helpful to them. The accreditation team visit was also an eye-opener. Staff commented that the questions that the team members asked caused them to reflect even further on the operations of the school and the need for some changes.

Day school directors must deal with the systemic implications of any changes in such areas as religious and educational philosophy as well as in the use of space and resources. If the school adds intramural sports with practice in the morning, will that interfere with the morning davening? If the school adds a community service component involving the delivery of food to the homeless or the aged, must the food be strictly kosher? If the middle school grades are placed in another building, how will that affect the use and placement of the library?

Although managing change in a large school can be complicated, the director may have the advantage of an administrative staff:

> Fortunately I have an assistant principal for general studies, an assistant principal for Jewish studies, a counselor

and other specialists, and an extremely competent office staff. While my schedule is very busy and I have many meetings to attend, others to mediate, there are many day-to-day details that I have comfortably delegated to others. I really have had the luxury to study, to think, to read, and to attend conferences. There are many changes happening in education today—in school restructuring, in new forms of assessment, in new instructional strategies, in uses of technology. I am now working on ways that these reforms may fit into our school. I am planning a staff retreat to discuss some of these issues.

Hebrew Colleges

Hebrew colleges have faced many calls for change in the last two decades, and so strong leadership and management skills are required to respond to the challenge. In addition to needing the constant improvements and refinements that are required of any educational enterprise, Hebrew colleges require change for extrinsic reasons: a reduction in the size of its traditional and historical constituency (the high school and college students who commute to its central location after their own school's classes are over for the day) and a reduction in allocations from local federations (a topic that is discussed in the next chapter). Thus in this type of institution, managing change is akin to managing viability and to the challenge of continuing to exist as an independent enterprise.

Executives in Hebrew colleges have managed programmatic changes in their institutions in a variety of ways, reflecting both their own experience and orientation and the choices made by their boards. Some of these colleges retain the formal educational components—the degree-granting programs—as their primary mission but focus increasingly on graduate rather than undergraduate programs, as in this situation:

> We have accepted BAs in other fields and from other institutions as entrance criteria for our graduate programs in Jewish education and Jewish studies. We have people who are teaching in religious schools or working in Jewish communal organizations who are interested in the graduate programs but who would not enroll in our college undergraduate program. We have had to adjust our approach, however, and teach more in English than in Hebrew.

Other Hebrew colleges have made the formal educational programs only a small part of the institution's daily operation. Instead, the college has become a major Jewish cultural center in the city as well a center for enrichment courses. An educator described such a situation:

> We have a major arts show every year, special exhibits on topics such as archaeology or historic manuscripts, and we put on a major academic conference each year. Don't get me wrong; the formal educational programs are the heart and soul of this institution, but these other events are critical to our survival. They are of course educational, but they are also good public relations, and we are able to get support from them for our other programs.

Such colleges have also found that one way to continue their educational mission is to "go where the people are":

> We used to be a centralized institution. Now most of our high school courses and some of our college and graduate

courses are given at branch locations not only in this city but in other areas as well. In this way we meet the needs of those communities, and we keep our faculty employed.

Managing change in a Hebrew college requires technical managerial skills, but it may also require the type of leader who can look beyond the traditional roles and mission of the organization.

Central Agencies

Central agencies also require the kind of leadership that can move an organization beyond its original structure and roles. As providers of information, technical assistance and training, special programs, and, in some cases, accreditation, they have a voluntary relationship with the schools they serve. They are intermediaries without governance or authoritative relationships with their clients; they are intermediaries between the federations and the schools. Increasingly, in order to survive, they have had to create a market for their services. One executive explained,

> We used to be the experts, and the schools came to us or subscribed to our standard setting. Years ago this organization made policy for the Hebrew schools in the region. It was almost like a school district's relationship with a school. That is no longer the case. The skills our staff needs now are very different from what they were years ago. They need human relations skills, the ability to "get into the school and sell the program and our services." Some of the schools don't want us, and unfortunately some of our sister agencies that receive funding from the federation don't want us around either. But we know we are performing services that are unduplicated in the area.

It is our job to make ourselves known and available. It is my job to get my staff into a collaborative mode with the clients.

Conclusion

In this chapter we have focused on the challenges facing educational executives as they try to manage change. Because renewal is a constant factor of good education, educational organizations would stagnate, shrink, or even disappear if the executives who served them did not have the capacity to lead and to manage change. Unfortunately, not all administrators have the skills to manage the change process effectively.

The following lessons were derived from the field interviews; it is hoped that they will assist in the consideration of the process of change:

1. Educational administrators must set aside time to think about their organization's goals and options for achieving them; they must think about a vision for the organization's future and a way of realizing it.
2. Vision is important, but it is not enough: the participation of others is vital to the process of change. In managing change, skills involving human relations are as important as substantive knowledge.
3. Good leaders use knowledge successfully; they know how to obtain the resources (the information and assistance) that will support the changes they envision, and they know that change need not cost a great deal of money.
4. Good leaders must consider and attend to the systemic implications of organizational changes.

5. Good leaders should acknowledge that changing their own organization might best be accomplished if they collaborate with sister organizations; they must realize that protecting their turf is likely to be a regressive act.

In Part Two we present several case vignettes that further amplify these issues.

Chapter 6

▼

MANAGING
FUNDS

Managing funds is essential to the management of material resources. Without skills in the management of funds, executives lack the power to lead; they lack the capacity to put into place the program and structures that they as leaders envision. In addition, managing funds is a critical component of managing human resources. This is most clear when it applies to decisions about hiring staff, allocating funds to staff positions, increasing or decreasing class size, purchasing materials for the staff, and planning programs for students with special needs. An executive's constituency will undoubtedly react to decisions about the way funds are allocated, and so the executive must possess strong human relations skills in order to mediate between competing demands and calm dissatisfied groups or individuals.

The interrelationship between the management of funds and the management of human resources is evident in another way. For most executives the process of acquiring funds requires strong interpersonal skills as well as financial and entrepreneurial skills. One must negotiate with a committee or a board (as in a congregational school), a set of boards (as in a consolidated school), funding agencies (such as federations), and alternative sources of funding (such as foundations). These processes are not purely rational facts-and-figures activities. The executive must get to know the funder, negotiate, and compromise—for example, with those competing for the same funds within the organization or within the community.

The ability to acquire and manage funds differs among individuals, according to their relative interests and experiences. But it also differs for executives according to the various contexts and the types of organizations that provide educational services. The nature of the organization can influence the degree to which the executive has control over the management of funds. Nonetheless, a skilled executive can strengthen or weaken that influence. The following discussion illustrates the dilemmas executives face in different settings.

Congregational Schools

As in many other arenas in which executive skills play a role, that of managing funds may be the most problematic and the most ambiguous for the director of a congregational school. Like the issues involved in managing change in a school that is not an independent entity, those involved in managing funds in such a school are complicated because the school must function within a larger system. The congregational school may raise funds with tuition and special fund-raising projects, but typically it is largely subsidized by the host congregation's budget. This significantly reduces the school executive's autonomy in managing the funds for the school. The executive may not even play a significant role in the process of allocating funds:

> Each year I sit down with the school committee chair, and we discuss the budget needs for the following year. The school committee chair then appears before the budget committee of the board. Sometimes I am part of that meeting and sometimes not. It has depended on the will of the school committee chair. In the end I have to make do with the will of the board. I do have a small discretionary fund for special needs or events, but it is only because I asked for and received a contribution from the sisterhood. Fortunately it has become a yearly gift, but that may change if their fund-raising changes.

A more experienced educational director has successfully increased his influence on the management of funds for the educational program:

> I prepare the budget request, although I do sit down with the school committee chair and sometimes with a team of faculty. I appear before the budget committee and the full board to defend my request, and I have successfully managed to get increases in funds for special programs. I have a special school bank account, and my secretary writes the checks. But the executive director of the temple signs the checks. However, I realize that many of my colleagues do not have this much control over their school funds.

A relatively weak role in funds management is viewed as a mixed blessing by some educational directors. On the one hand, they may feel they have little control over some decisions about the school and the resources available to it. On the other hand, they may feel relieved not to be involved with fund-raising as a major activity. One educational director said,

> I am glad not to have to worry about raising tuition, nego-tiating with federations, attending fund-raising events, and so on. I'm not sure I would be good at it anyway. True, I sometimes have to plead with the board for an additional teacher, but I can spend most of my time managing the school on a day-to-day basis, working with teachers, parents, and kids. I prefer doing that.

Yet others realize that their inability to manage and control school funds has been a barrier to the improvement and development of the school. For example, one administrator said,

> I have wanted to do some radical restructuring of this religious school. I am in a graduate program now, and I am really excited about applying what I have learned about school reform in this setting. But I need a backer. I am trying to convince some of the well-to-do parents to finance some of the proposed changes, but it will probably have to go to the board anyway.

Day Schools

Day school directors typically have more control over the management of funds for their schools, but they also face the challenges of raising funds and working with inadequate funding. Funds are raised by means of tuition, contributions, fund-raising activities, and federation allocations. Some day schools have a director of development, who relieves the educational director of some fund-raising responsibilities. The board of directors also plays a role in the processes of raising and managing funds, but the director implements fiscal policy.

The role of the administrator in raising and managing funds can depend on the school's stage in its life cycle. In a small school or in one that is struggling financially, the director may spend a great deal of time in this arena, as this administrator reports:

> I spend a lot of time juggling the books, asking for dona-tions, and trying to encourage some of the wealthier people in the community to get active in the school. Unfor-tunately, they get courted by the federation and other more prestigious organizations in the community. It is hard to get them to be strong supporters and lay leaders of the school.

Some day schools have become large and successful and require full-time financial management. When a board of directors hires a full-time business manager, the educational director has fewer day-to-day managerial responsibilities but may continue to be involved in budget hearings at the federation. This, too, has been viewed as a mixed blessing by some executives. One said,

> Where there is money, there is power. And someone else who is responsible to the board is managing the money. We have an ambiguous relationship because he is not my boss, and I am not his. We still have to work out the kinks in this arrangement.

The cost of day school education continues to rise. Some schools are facing critical periods because they have reached the maximum tuition levels that families can tolerate. The federations are struggling with their own fund-raising problems and cannot subsidize the day schools at higher levels. Day school directors are only beginning to look for alternative sources of funding, such as special grants and public and private sources. Lack of funds and high costs can be particularly stressful to the Jewish educator because of the high value placed on providing intensive Jewish education to all who want it, regardless of the ability to pay.

Hebrew Colleges, Central Agencies, and Jewish Community Centers

Historically many Jewish communal agencies have depended on communal funds for their existence. Years ago it was not unusual for Hebrew colleges and central agencies to acquire more than 90 percent of their funds from the federations. Jewish community centers were also major recipients of federation funding. But times are changing. Increasingly, the executives of these agencies must not only manage their agencies' operating funds but also seek and acquire new sources of funding. A successful candidate for director or president of a Hebrew college or even for director of a central agency must demonstrate fund-raising capabilities.

Some executives have demonstrated strong entrepreneurial skills and have successfully managed the transition from relying mainly on communal funds to obtaining most of their funding from other sources. Said one college director,

> We now get only 30 percent of the funds for this Hebrew college from the federation. The rest is raised from tuition, and especially from tuition from our adult education enrichment program, fund-raising activities and donors, and a variety of special grants. I spend a lot of my time learning about and writing grants.

Some central agencies are seeking grants as well as charging fees for special kinds of services.

A particular problem for many administrators is managing organizations with decreasing funds. Sometimes the decline in funding is caused by federation cutbacks, but other times there are unpredicted shortfalls in revenue. These may be caused by a reversal in enrollment and therefore in tuition revenues, the expiration of special grants, or a recession-induced reduction in donations. One executive commented,

> We had to do a big budget revision in midyear because of a shortfall in revenue. I had to lay off some administrative and support staff as well as some part-time teachers. The rest of us took on additional responsibilities. People are very nervous, and I suppose morale is low. But I tell them that we are not the only ones in this predicament.

Conclusion

Managing organizations with declining funds is probably the best example of the need to manage human resources carefully. In this chapter we have described some of the challenges educational administrators face in their role as managers of funds. Not every administrator has been trained for or is comfortable with such a challenge. The following lessons derived from the field interviews may assist in thinking about the process of managing funds:

1. Managing funds requires entrepreneurial and business skills as well as skills in managing human resources.
2. Because decisions about funds distribution have ramifications for other components of the educational system, a successful funds manager must think systemically. For Jewish educators

these ramifications may be particularly stressful because of an unwillingness to deny a quality Jewish education to all children, regardless of the family's ability to pay.

3. As traditional sources of funding sources change, the successful administrator must seek alternative sources.

In Part Two we present several case vignettes that further amplify these issues.

PART TWO
THE CASE VIGNETTES

INSTRUCTIONS FOR USING THE CASE VIGNETTES

Part Two of this volume consists of case vignettes that can be used for teaching groups or individuals. Each vignette focuses on one or more dilemmas in managing human and/or material resources. Some of the vignettes illustrate problems encountered by administrators for which there is no described solution. Others illustrate problems and attempted solutions. About one fourth of the cases can be described as "solution" cases.

Each case vignette illustrates at least one leadership skill area. The vignettes have been clustered according to the primary skill areas that the cases illustrate. Each case and the questions that follow it are numbered in sequential order. The cases are preceded by a Table of Contents of Case Vignettes by Skill Areas (p. 85). To aid in the selection of appropriate case vignettes, we have noted additional case numbers that may be used as secondary sources to illustrate the skill areas.

All the vignettes include questions for reflection, discussion, and analysis. First, there is a set of general questions on problem solving, designed to enhance the decision-making and problem-solving skills of leaders and managers in education. If the vignette includes an attempted solution to a problem, there are questions regarding both the problem and the solution. The general problem-solving questions are as follows:

1. What are the key issues or problems in this case?
   If the case presents a solution, also ask, What were the guiding principles that appeared to contribute to the way the problem was solved?

2. Given the limited amount of information, what assumptions need to be made?

3. What options would you consider using to address the situation described in this case?

4. Which option would you pick, and why?

5. How would you implement the option you selected?

6. What are the potential consequences should your option be implemented?

In addition, there is a question about the guiding principles that have influenced your choice of solutions:

7. What are the guiding principles that contributed to your selection of these options?

The ten guiding principles were presented in Chapter 1; they are (1) mission, (2) planning, (3) accountability, (4) reflective practice, (5) respect, (6) flexibility, (7) maintenance of professional demeanor, (8) concerns about the physical environment, (9) fiscal responsibility, and (10) Jewish values. Their definitions are repeated for the reader's review on page 89. The preceding general problem-solving questions are designed to be used with all the case vignettes.

In addition to the general questions on problem solving, each vignette includes at least two specific and focused questions that are meant to stimulate analysis and discussion of the case itself. These questions are designed to enhance reflection on and discussion of the specific skill area illustrated in the vignette. If the cases are used in a group setting with a facilitator or an instructor, the facilitator or instructor should certainly consider adding or substituting other focused discussion questions.

Learning by the Case Method

The case vignettes can be used by individual readers who reflect on their problem-solving skills and on the way they carry out their roles, by small groups engaged in informal study and analysis, or by groups in a formal in-service or classroom setting led by an instructor. Although group study has been found to be advantageous and the case method has been found to be particularly useful in a group setting, individuals can also learn a great deal by reading, and carefully analyzing, the cases. Many individuals will find that they face situations similar to those presented in the case vignettes. They may benefit enormously by reflecting on the problems presented in the cases, using the general questions and the discussion questions as a guide. As an aid for both the individual and the group user, a set of potential solutions is presented for the first case in each of the skill areas.

When using the cases in a formal group setting, remember

that teaching by the case method requires the instructor or facilitator to lead an effective group discussion. While the responsibility for learning rests with the participants, the responsibility for teaching rests with the instructor or facilitator, who guides the learners through a series of questions designed to uncover the basic principles within a case. The instructional process moves through the following steps:

1. describing and understanding the situation
2. clarifying unclear aspects of the situation
3. analyzing and interpreting
4. evaluating

One approach for using the questions for discussion includes three steps:

1. Each student reads the case individually.
2. For each discussion question, students offer a response, and each response is listed on the chalkboard.
3. The instructor leads a general discussion on the question, beginning with the students' responses.

A second approach is one in which the class is divided into small groups of two or three individuals. The members of a group work together for approximately twenty minutes, going through the questions and coming up with alternative solutions to the issues. Each group then presents its conclusions to the class, and a class discussion may follow.

It is important to note that there may be no one preferred solution. One option or a combination of options may be viable. The key factor is engaging in the problem-solving process, either in a group or individually.

Teaching by the Case Method

In preparing this volume, we invited a group of educators to review and "field test" a sample of case vignettes, discuss the general questions on problem solving, and generate several viable options for addressing the situations described in the vignettes. The suggested options for each case that they discussed are included immediately after that case.*

To illustrate the outcome of the process (the type of responses that the general questions generated and that were listed on the chalkboard—as outlined in step 2, described above), the results of a sample case are presented here.

Managing Change

Case 8 ▼ The Price of Change
Imposed from the Top

Middletown has a community Hebrew school. For nearly twenty years the city's three congregations (Orthodox, Conservative, and Reform) have agreed that the central agency would run a Hebrew language program while each congregation would run its own religious school and program for the primary grades. The titular head of the community school is also the executive director of the central agency.

According to the executive director, the congregations hold that the community Hebrew school is necessary

---

* These educators included two professors of Jewish education with extensive experience in schools and in supervision (Dr. Diane King and Dr. Saul Wachs), one headmaster of a large day school (Dr. Steven M. Brown), one educational director of a congregational school (Rabbi Cynthia Kravitz), and one student in the Masters in Jewish Education program at Gratz College (Arlyne Unger).

because the individual congregations have neither the qualified personnel to run a school nor the resources to administer one, given the diminishing number of Jewish school-age children in the congregations. Attendance at the school is a prerequisite for a bar or bat mitzvah ceremony at any of the three synagogues. Parents accept the necessity of this arrangement but view the community Hebrew school as a "bitter pill" that their children must take in order to have a bar or bat mitzvah.

The community Hebrew school serves about 140 students, who meet twice a week for a total of four hours a week, beginning in the fourth grade and continuing through the seventh, the year of their bar or bat mitzvah. The executive director and the teachers of the seventh graders were concerned about two problems: the lack of attendance during the fourth year of the program and the dropout rate once students had become b'nai mitzvah. These factors reflected a generally negative attitude toward the fourth year of learning and left students who remained in the program with a sense of alienation.

The executive director responded by proposing to the board of trustees a realignment and a restructuring of the community Hebrew school. He proposed a model in which the students would begin their studies in the third grade and attend the school through the sixth grade. The seventh grade would be optional, for those students who wished to continue their studies in the Hebrew program; for most students, however, the seventh grade would be reserved for bar or bat mitzvah instruction plus religious school. The board of the central agency approved the plan and suggested that it be presented to the three congregations.

The executive director obtained the support of all the rabbis and then brought the restructuring plan to the religious-education committees of the three congregations. One congregation sent a survey to the families affected by the change, in order to elicit a better understanding of its congregants' attitude toward the issue. The other congregations made a decision either in committee or in a conference of the rabbi and the chairperson of the religious education committee. In these two congregations, parents at large were not consulted, nor were most of them aware of the changes being sought.

In the spring the three congregations ratified the restructuring, and all parents were informed of the change. Shortly afterward a groundswell of negative reaction arose from a number of parents, threatening to undermine the entire project. Congregants, angry about what they perceived as an imposed change, held private meetings. A group of parents called a meeting to which the executive director and the president of the central agency were invited. At this meeting they brought up issues beyond the one of beginning Hebrew school in the third grade. The parents complained that the school dictated policies without requesting their advice or taking into account their feelings, and they were "fed up."

The Results of an Illustrative Group Discussion

In response to Case 8, participants in the sample group discussion asked the questions, and presented the solutions, below:
1. What are the key issues or problems in this case?
    • People affected by a change must be involved in the decision-

making process and must be given ownership of both the problems and the solutions.

- Information about why the parents and the students were dissatisfied was lacking.
- Mechanisms for systemic feedback from the parents were lacking.
- Prevailing issues of turf, control, and authority abounded.

2. Given the limited amount of information, what assumptions need to be made?
   - There were problems in the school, albeit they were inadequately understood.
   - The leaders of the central agency thought they had enough information to make the decisions.
   - The leadership was not aware of the extent of the parents' dissatisfaction with the community school.
   - The change instituted by the leaders of the central agency was just the straw that broke the camel's back. Apparently a pattern of not involving all those affected by a decision had already developed.

3. What options would you consider using to address the situation described in this case?
   Note: The group generated a greater number of options than those presented here and then narrowed them down to these three:
   - It may be best to put the changes on hold and engage in a more sophisticated long-range planning process that would involve all constituencies (parents, educators, rabbis, and lay leaders of the congregations) in defining the problems and choosing the solutions.
   - Convene separate focus groups of parents, students, and teachers to explain the plan and to discuss perceptions of

the school's goals, its problems, and participants' reactions to the new plan. Based on the results of these meetings, the plan could be continued, discarded, or modified.

- Implement the changes in the seventh grade, and mount a public relations effort to begin the midweek classes in the third grade.

4. Which option would you pick, and why?
   Note: To illustrate a sequence of thoughts on the issue, the remaining answers are based on the selection of the first option. This should not be considered the only option, however.

5. How would you implement the option you selected?
   - Seek an outside consultant, who would help organize the planning process, create a steering committee made up of representatives of all the constituencies, maintain a public approach to the process, and make it an extraordinary event in the life of the community.

6. What are the potential consequences should your option be implemented?
   - Participants will become partners in understanding the problems, and they will buy into the solutions. They may then use the expertise they have gained in helping the school and the community solve their problems. On the other hand, the executive director may not approve of the decisions and may resign.

7. What are the guiding principles that contributed to your selection of this option?
   - Mission. The school should work hard at deciding what its mission is and then base a planning process on it.

- Planning. People who are affected by the decisions are engaged in the planning process.
- Accountability. Those responsible for the school are held accountable for an unpopular decision. With a community-based decision, everyone is held accountable.
- Jewish values. Parents are responsible for their children's education. The original process ignored the parents' role as their children's primary educators.

The group of educators that generated the preceding conclusions carried out this process for eleven cases. The options for solutions they generated are included in this volume. The table of contents indicates the cases for which solutions are provided. The cases for which solutions are presented represent each skill area that is included in this casebook; they are also examples of dilemmas faced by educators in different settings: day schools, congregational schools, Jewish family service organizations, the institutions of the different denominations, and institutions of various sizes.

The options are presented for illustrative purposes only, to assist the individual reader who may be searching for solutions and to demonstrate the potential outcomes of an effective group discussion. In considering the solutions, it is important to note that the authors are not recommending any particular solution or combination of options. In most cases in real life, the range of options available to a leader is wide, and the reader may generate alternative suggestions to the ones posed here. Often there is more than one acceptable option that may yield good results. It is important to note, however, that sometimes a particular answer may be wrong. Allowing a dispute between staff members to fester or failing to answer reasonable questions posed by the lay leadership may reflect bad leadership and mismanagement. The guiding principles can be an important yardstick by which to measure the solutions.

Table of Contents
Case Vignettes by Skill Area

---

* Suggested options or solutions are presented at the end of the case.
† Cases in italics may be considered secondary illustrations of the skill area.

---

* Suggested options or solutions are presented at the end of the case.

---

* Suggested options or solutions are presented at the end of the case.

General Questions for
All Case Vignettes

1. What are the key issues or problems in this case?
    If the case presents a solution, also ask, What were the guiding principles that appeared to contribute to the way the problem was solved?

2. Given the limited amount of information, what assumptions need to be made?

3. What options would you consider using to address the situation described in this case?

4. Which option would you pick, and why?

5. How would you implement the option you selected?

6. What are the potential consequences should your option be implemented?

7. What are the guiding principles that contributed to your selection of this option?

The Guiding Principles of Leadership Practices

1. **Mission.** Goals derived from the institution's statement of mission should drive managerial practice.

2. **Planning.** Careful planning of all aspects of educational activity is essential for success.

3. **Accountability.** Executives should hold themselves and others accountable, linking desired behavioral ends to plans based on goals and standards.

4. **Reflective practice.** Managerial practice should be guided by an analysis and understanding of both the dynamics of the organization and the dynamics of the personalities of the individuals.

5. **Respect.** Managerial practice and behaviors should clearly demonstrate respect for students, staff, parents, other professionals, and lay leaders.

6. **Flexibility.** Flexibility is essential for effective educational and administrative practice.

7. **Maintenance of professional demeanor.** The executive should separate his or her professional and private lives and not attend to private business or show personal biases while carrying out professional responsibilities.

8. **Concerns about the physical environment.** The quality of the environment contributes to the educational experience and can facilitate or hinder that experience.

9. **Fiscal responsibility.** The organization cannot function without responsible fiscal practices, including the continuous monitoring of budgets.

10. **Jewish values.** For Jewish educators adherence to Jewish values is the backbone of leadership and management.

THE CASE
VIGNETTES

Defining Vision and Setting Goals

Case 1 ▼ Laying Off Teachers*

Dr. Susan Davis is an experienced day school director with credentials in Jewish and general education. When she began in her current position, she had a vision of a school that would exemplify excellence in general and Jewish studies and where both students and staff would be excited by and engaged in the learning process. Although she knew content to be crucial, she was also concerned about the emotional well-being of the children. According to her vision, students would graduate as knowledgeable and committed Jews, prepared to continue their education in high school and strongly concerned about social and humanitarian issues affecting Jews and others. To achieve this, she envisioned the school as a caring environment for students and staff members.

Dr. Davis felt that over the years she had successfully facilitated curriculum development, trained the staff in instructional strategies, and supported teachers in their efforts to develop themselves professionally. She was able to structure her time so that she could concentrate on assisting the staff. Although the school's rules required the formal evaluation of teachers (twice a year for new teachers; at least every two years for others), Dr. Davis considered classroom observations to be primarily opportunities to provide teachers with feedback and coaching.

Dr. Davis faced a major dilemma. For the fourth grade Hebrew class, she had hired Rachel Singer, a woman who had formerly taught in a traditional yeshiva setting. Mrs. Singer was described

---

* This vignette can also be used to illustrate the skill area of Managing Staff.

as "a truly fine person and an observant and committed Jew." During the interview Dr. Davis emphasized that her school was a community day school with a strong focus on what might be called liberal humanitarian values. "Our Tanach curriculum emphasizes social values, and we try to plan interdisciplinary lessons—for example, with social studies and the book of Judges. This requires taking a broad perspective on the text and coordinating with other teachers in the school." Mrs. Singer said that she understood what was required.

After the first six weeks of school, Dr. Davis observed Mrs. Singer's class. She was disappointed to find that Mrs. Singer was teaching the text mechanically, using only traditional commentary. Although the children were learning the verses and the text, there was little or no application of the ideas according to the prescribed curriculum. Dr. Davis later learned that Mrs. Singer had consulted briefly with the social studies teacher but had not carried the discussion further. The social studies teacher felt she ought to give Mrs. Singer "some space"—she should be available to help her, but she shouldn't push her too hard.

Dr. Davis met with Mrs. Singer, and they discussed the lesson. It became clear that Mrs. Singer was not comfortable with the innovative approach and did not really know how to implement it. Dr. Davis worked with her on setting goals for the lessons and devising strategies by which to achieve the goals. She pointed out resources the teacher could use and suggested that Mrs. Singer observe other teachers in the school. She also suggested that Mrs. Singer select a teacher with whom she felt comfortable, someone who might assist her in planning her curriculum.

By midyear there was little improvement in Mrs. Singer's approach or in the classroom's energy level. Mrs. Singer said she was trying but the method did not come to her naturally. Dr. Davis tried not to "crowd her," but she did inform the teacher that she had until May to work on the problem. "We will give you all the help we can, but you need to work on these changes."

Dr. Davis finally decided not to rehire Mrs. Singer, but she felt terrible about it. "It was such a tough decision. She is such a fine person. I don't remember ever terminating such a fine person before. I didn't know what else I could do."

See pages 88–89 for General Questions for All Case Vignettes and for The Guiding Principles of Leadership Practices.

Additional Discussion Questions for This Case

1. Did Dr. Davis contribute to Mrs. Singer's failure to succeed by giving her too much latitude?
2. Why was the decision so tough for Dr. Davis?
3. To what extent would a formal orientation and an in-service training program have been helpful in this situation? Why?

Suggested Options

1. It may take as long as a year for a new teacher to learn the culture of a school and to get to know which teachers to trust and consult. Given the scarcity of qualified day school teachers who are knowledgeable in *Tanach*, Dr. Davis may have been shortsighted in not allowing Mrs. Singer another year in which to adapt to the work environment, with additional assistance.

   Dr. Davis took upon herself a great deal of the work in advising this teacher. It might have been advisable for her to appoint another experienced teacher, for pay if necessary, to serve as Mrs. Singer's mentor and peer coach. This might have been less threatening than having the supervisor-evaluator in that role. The mentor-peer coach could have regularly reviewed Mrs. Singer's lesson plans, discussing with her the possibilities for emphasizing social values in each text. The two could also have team-taught some sessions, affording the opportunity for Mrs. Singer to observe the mentor-peer coach. Dr. Davis could have retained Mrs. Singer for another year on probation. She could have required her to take a summer course or a workshop series and to work one-on-one with the director or another mentor-teacher who had the time to devote to the new teacher.

2. Dr. Davis should consider eliciting more information from potential teachers during the interviewing and hiring process. For example, she should have asked Mrs. Singer about her motivation for teaching in the school and about her philosophy and attitudes regarding the teaching of Jewish texts. She could have asked for sample lesson plans and, if possible, observed the applicant in a teaching situation.

3. Dr. Davis probably handled the case just right, given her vision for the school. Given the amount of support and the number of suggestions she gave Mrs. Singer during the school year, it is probably better that she cut the cord sooner rather than let the situation continue into another year, when she might have developed a personal relationship with Mrs. Singer that might then have affected her professional responsibilities.

Defining Vision and Setting Goals

Case 2 ▼ How Do You Teach Morality?*

Jonathan Prince is the headmaster of a community day school that serves the seventh through twelfth grades in a midwestern city. He has been at the school for nine years and prides himself on his open relationship and good rapport with both staff and students. He encourages innovation, teacher-initiated programs, and shared decision making, and he keeps the staff well informed of all that is going on. When you ask teachers their opinion of the headmaster, the most frequent comment is, "He is a wonderful principal, an effective leader, and he treats us like professionals." Students also have positive feelings toward Mr. Prince, and the more insightful students say, "He treats the students with respect."

The school is generally a hubbub of activity. There are always projects in process or being planned. Each year a major project for the tenth grade is an extensive class trip, very often to New York, Boston, or Washington, D.C. Because of the high cost of such a trip and because of the educational value of students' assuming responsibility for themselves, the school has maintained a tradition that students engage in projects to raise money for the trip. One of the most successful of these projects is the sale of pizza in the school cafeteria. A student committee is responsible for managing the project, including managing the funds. After the "pizza project" had been successfully under way for several months, a committee consisting of students and their faculty adviser was surprised to find that the amount of money earned was not as great as they had assumed it to be. After several days of investigation, it

---

* This vignette can also be used to illustrate the skill area of Relating to Parents and Students.

was revealed that three students on the committee had been stealing from the pizza fund.

The faculty adviser brought the matter to Mr. Prince's attention. What should they do? This was a big problem for Mr. Prince, who put a high value on honesty and trust.

See pages 88–89 for General Questions for All Case Vignettes and for The Guiding Principles of Leadership Practices.

Additional Discussion Questions for This Case

1. How should the headmaster help the faculty adviser deal with the allegation? Should he involve only the three students or all the students in the school?
2. What practices or policies might guide Mr. Prince in confronting this situation?
3. How public should the process be? Why?

Defining Vision and Setting Goals

Case 3 ▼ A Struggle for Standards*

Arlene Feldman, an experienced educator, has spent ten years as the educational director of a Conservative congregation located in the suburbs of a major metropolitan area. The school enrolls about three hundred students each year. A persistent issue for Ms. Feldman has been the maintenance of academic standards in the departments of the school that are independent of bar or bat mitzvah instruction. As she stated, "While we obviously teach the reading of Hebrew, I put great emphasis on the teaching of biblical texts, the Jewish life cycle, the holidays . . . ." The school policy is that bar and bat mitzvah instruction is not part of the regular class curriculum but is taught by the cantor outside regular school hours.

Ms. Feldman's insistence on high academic standards has brought the school recognition for its accomplishments during her tenure as principal. For example, this year the United Synagogue cited the school for excellence, and four of its students advanced to the national level of the United Synagogue's Bible competition. "But," says Ms. Feldman,

> not everyone in the school likes to hear about emphasizing academics. They say, "After all, it is just Hebrew school." There are those who think of it as a bar mitzvah school. For example, I am often asked to "look the other way" and have the cantor work with the child at four o'clock on the day of Hebrew school and let the child come in late to class (regular classes begin at four-fifteen)

---

* This vignette can also be used to illustrate the skill areas of Relating to Parents and Students and Relating to Other Professionals in One's Organization.

in order to avoid an extra driving day. I always say no, stressing the importance of the regular school curriculum, and suggest that they send the child in a cab on the non-Hebrew-school day if necessary.

This situation is exacerbated by the cantor, who, Ms. Feldman claims, sometimes "sneaks children out of class" for a bar or bat mitzvah lesson, either for his own convenience or because the parents are his friends. Ms. Feldman has had several run-ins with the cantor on this issue, and in retaliation he has told the school board that the children "don't know how to read well enough, and it takes more time to prepare them."

See pages 88–89 for General Questions for All Case Vignettes and for The Guiding Principles of Leadership Practices.

Additional Discussion Questions for This Case

1. Who could play a third party role in mediating the differences between Ms. Feldman and the cantor?
2. How could the relationship between the principal and the cantor be improved?
3. How might the educational director determine whether her standards are too high?
4. How might the school policies and missions be more widely promoted in the school community?
5. What are the pitfalls of Ms. Feldman's attitudes toward her students' parents? What are the pitfalls of her attitudes toward the cantor?
6. What are the strengths of Ms. Feldman's struggle for standards? What are the weaknesses?
7. How might this case have differed if the school were a consolidated school? If it were a day school?

Defining Roles

Case 4 ▾ Jewish Family Life Education: The Jewish Family Service Perspective*

In this small city the Jewish family service (JFS) is a small agency whose four-person staff is housed in the Jewish community center (JCC), along with the office of the federation of Jewish agencies. Under the leadership of its current director, the JFS made several changes in its mission and programs. In addition to maintaining its traditional role of social service, the agency began a program on Jewish Family Life Education (JFLE), providing services to other Jewish organizations in the community on social issues and life cycle events. But in the early years of this initiative, the agency had to struggle to get the program off the ground. "We had to beg institutions to let us in," said the director.

When Sue Klein, who holds master's degrees in education and social work, joined the agency, the director had high hopes that the JFLE program would be revitalized under her leadership. In the beginning Ms. Klein struggled to market JFLE. Little by little, however, she made inroads. As a new person in the agency, she was able to begin working with the local day school, overcoming a bad experience the school had had with the agency several years before. For third through eighth graders, she negotiated a program to provide workshops on substance abuse, peer pressure, and other issues pertinent to the students. Working through the principals and with the support of the rabbis, she also gained access to the two main religious schools, obtaining permission to conduct workshops for the students on the meaning of becoming a bar or bat mitzvah and on other issues relating to adolescence.

---

* This vignette can also be used to illustrate the skill areas of Relating to Other Professionals in One's Organization and Managing Oneself.

The JFLE program really began to take off after a new rabbi came to the Conservative congregation. He had worked successfully with the JFS in his former community and was interested in expanding the program further. Coincidentally, before his arrival Ms. Klein had become especially involved in the Conservative synagogue and in Jewish study and practice. Her workshops with bar and bat mitzvah students gained added meaning when she embarked on an adult bat mitzvah program.

Ms. Klein and the new rabbi planned several joint ventures, including a series of workshops for expectant parents that dealt with both Jewish ritual and the social and emotional aspects of becoming a parent. Gradually and with the assistance of the JFS director, Ms. Klein learned to improve the programs, for example, by securing the involvement of planning committees in the participating organizations. She also received help from a new and revitalized JFLE committee appointed by the JFS board. As a result of these events, the JFLE program has become a well used and highly regarded resource in the community, particularly in synagogues and in the day school.

Nonetheless, Ms. Klein continues to have difficulty gaining access to some other organizations. For example, a session planned with Hadassah members on communication in a Jewish marriage never took place. The biggest frustration is the difficulty of getting the teen director of the Jewish community center to cooperate with the current JFLE priority: greater involvement with the teenage population. Even though the new director of the JCC has voiced support for the program, Ms. Klein has been unable to establish a relationship with the teen director. She says, "This is something I am struggling with, trying to figure out how to work through his resistance. It is so ironic that I am making greater headway in the religious schools than with my neighbor in this federation-supported setting."

See pages 88–89 for General Questions for All Case Vignettes and for The Guiding Principles of Leadership Practices.

Additional Discussion Questions for This Case

1. Why was Ms. Klein having difficulty making inroads in the teen program? Why had she been more successful in the synagogues and in the day school?
2. What can she do to overcome the resistance to JFLE? Is there something she did in the synagogues and in the day school that she neglected to do in her work with the other organizations?

Suggested Options

1. Ms. Klein and the teen director should meet to discuss the reasons for the teen director's resistance the JFLE program and to get to the root of the problem, which may be a personality clash, a fear that the JFLE program is encroaching on the JCC's turf, or the teen director's lack of comfort with the substance of the JFLE program.
2. Ms. Klein could enlist the support of the JFS director and suggest a meeting of the directors of both agencies (the JFC and the JCC) to discuss cooperation between the two agencies. Such a meeting could be followed up with a meeting of the two agencies' directors and staff to jointly plan the JFLE teen program in conjunction with the JCC's teen activities, thereby giving more ownership of the program to the JCC.
3. The JFS and the JCC could undertake a joint-needs assessment to determine the needs of the teenage population and how Ms. Klein and her agency's services can or should address those needs.

Defining Roles

Case 5 ▾ Making Room for More Curriculum Content*

David Michaels was hired by an affluent southern California congregation with the mission of solving a problem. For several years the supplementary school had been adding pieces to its curriculum in an effort to satisfy the interests of different groups within the congregation. The congregation had an active and concerned parent body that had a great many ideas about what the religious school should offer. Simply stated, there was not enough time to meet all the objectives that had been adopted and accommodate all the specialists involved. Either some objectives would have to go, or class time would have to be increased substantially in order cover everything. But Mr. Michaels was sure that either solution would be difficult to implement.

Mr. Michaels realized he had to devise a process for solving the school's problem that would involve all the key players and satisfy them that their interests had been taken into account. First he got the education committee to work with him. They took these steps:

1. They surveyed parents to determine their needs and interests.
2. They surveyed students to find out what they thought of the current curriculum.
3. They documented the results of both surveys in a mailing to all members of the congregation.
4. They presented the synagogue's board with a solution that

---

* This vignette can also be used to illustrate the skill areas of Managing Change and Relating to Other Professionals in One's Organization.

called for increasing the number of school hours per week to accommodate a net gain of one hour of Hebrew instruction and thirty minutes of religious school.

5. They made presentations to the parents, explaining why an increase in time was the best solution.

Mr. Michaels acknowledged that this was a very time-consuming process and that he fielded "some tough questions and objections" along the way. When the new schedule was instituted, however, there were no complaints from parents, teachers, or students, and the change was accomplished very smoothly.

See pages 88–89 for General Questions for All Case Vignettes and for The Guiding Principles of Leadership Practices.

Additional Discussion Questions for This Case

1. If the overload problem was so obvious, why didn't Mr. Michaels simply state the problem in writing, consult with a few of the key actors, develop options, and then involve board? What would the advantages or disadvantages of this approach have been?

2. Is the fact that Mr. Michaels seems to present his solution a weakness?

Defining Roles

Case 6 ▼ Defining One's Role: Agency Director or Jewish Educator?*

Because of her primary commitment to the Jewish community and to her Jewish identity, Naomi Bailey, an MSW, chose to pursue her career within the framework of a Jewish family service agency. Her first job was in a large agency, where she became attuned to disagreements about how "Jewish" the agency should be. For example, leaders and members of the nearby Orthodox community were reluctant to use the agency's services because they felt the agency lacked sensitivity to their concerns. Only after the agency hired an Orthodox social worker did the clients from that community begin to use its services.

After six years Ms. Bailey became director of a small Jewish family service agency located in a small, affluent exurban community. Her staff consisted of two part-time social workers and a full-time secretary. From the beginning she saw her role as agency director and Jewish educator and sought to define the agency's Jewishness. Much to the surprise of her board, she began her tenure in the position by attaching mezuzahs to the doorposts of the agency's offices. Contrary to previous agency policy, she also insisted that no nonkosher food be served at any agency-sponsored activities.

One of her major challenges as agency director and Jewish educator was in the hiring and supervising of the staff. The challenge began in the hiring process. Since it is illegal to discriminate

---

* This vignette can also be used to illustrate the skill areas of Managing Lay-Professional Relations and Managing Day-to-Day Operations.

in hiring, the agency's classified advertisements read, "Knowledge of Judaism required." Ms. Bailey commented, "When I interview workers, I examine their feelings about Judaism. I don't care if it is Orthodox, Conservative, Reform. I want to know about their values, their attitudes about parenting, raising children in an intermarried family, their knowledge of the Jewish approach to things like social responsibility to parents and grandparents."

Ms. Bailey extends her emphasis on Jewish morality to the therapy situation. This approach was discussed in the context of supervision:

> We are a small staff, so we do peer supervision, every week for one hour. Although I only hire serious, self-motivated workers who can work on their own, we do a lot of discussion of each case. After intake, we decide as a group if the client is appropriate for our agency. And we discuss the Jewish/moral dimension of a case. For example, one client was dealing with the issue and problems of caring for elderly parents. She had a lot of ambivalence about it and agonized a great deal about the burden. I suggested to the worker that she describe the talmudic approach to responsibility for parents. A Freudian approach is not enough. We have a special mission.

See pages 88–89 for General Questions for All Case Vignettes and for The Guiding Principles of Leadership Practices.

Additional Discussion Questions for This Case

1. What are the strengths of Ms. Bailey's approach to dealing with her staff? What are the strengths of her approach to dealing with the "Jewishness" of the agency?

2. What are the weaknesses of Ms. Bailey's approach to dealing with her staff? What are the weaknesses of her approach to dealing with the "Jewishness" of the agency?

3. How might her situation been different in an urban community? How might it have been different in a suburban community?

Defining Roles

Case 7 ▾ Managing Growth: We Grew Too Fast

Rabbi Levin is vice-principal of a growing Solomon Schechter day school of 240 students. He was hired with the general mandate of overseeing the Jewish studies program, but his actual responsibilities were not clearly defined. After three years in the position, he was still grappling with the way responsibilities were apportioned among himself, the principal, and other staff members.

The school started off small and quickly established a "homey, family-like" culture. The staff and administration made decisions somewhat casually. Although teachers had a great deal of autonomy, there was a lot of spirit and a sense of staff ownership of the school, and "it worked." To a large extent the operation of the school was overseen by the secretary, who was the quintessential Jewish mother, and by the principal, who was always available to listen to the smallest complaint or request.

Now, however, the school has grown too large to be run like a family. The board and the principal realize this, but as yet no one has taken on the role of trying to reformulate the approach to running the school. Rabbi Levin feels the issue is becoming more critical not only for his role but for the school, yet he does not feel he has the knowledge or the skills to initiate changes. Nor is he sure he has the authority to do so. He is wondering what he should do.

See pages 88–89 for General Questions for All Case Vignettes and for The Guiding Principles of Leadership Practices.

Additional Discussion Questions for This Case

1. How might the problems associated with rapid growth have become obvious to the board and the principal?
2. What authority does Rabbi Levin need to initiate change?
3. What practices might help Rabbi Levin with the process of change?
4. How might a strategic plan or a long-range planning process help here?
5. Does homeyness negate good organizational planning and structure?

Managing Change

Case 8 ▼ The Price of Change Imposed from the Top*

Middletown has a community Hebrew school. For nearly twenty years the city's three congregations (Orthodox, Conservative, and Reform) have agreed that the central agency should run a Hebrew-language program while each congregation would run its own religious school and program for the primary grades. The titular head of the school is also the executive director of the central agency.

According to the director, the congregations hold that the community Hebrew school is necessary because the individual congregations have neither the qualified personnel to run a school nor the resources to administer one, given the diminishing number of Jewish school-age children in the community. Attendance at the school is a prerequisite for a bar or bat mitzvah ceremony at any of the three synagogues. Parents accept the necessity of this arrangement but view the community Hebrew school as a "bitter pill" that their children must take in order to have a bar or bat mitzvah.

The community Hebrew school serves about 140 students, who meet twice a week for a total of four hours a week, beginning in the fourth grade and continuing through the seventh, the year of their bar or bat mitzvah. The executive director and the teachers of the seventh graders were concerned about two problems: the lack of attendance during the fourth year of the program and the dropout rate once the students had become b'nai mitzvah. These

---

* This vignette can also be used to illustrate the skill areas of Adjusting Vision and Setting Goals, and Relating to Parents and Students.

factors reflected a generally negative attitude toward the fourth year of learning and left students who remained in the program with a sense of alienation.

The executive director responded by proposing to the board of trustees a realignment and restructuring of the community Hebrew school. He proposed a model in which the students would begin their studies in the third grade and attend the school through the sixth grade. The seventh grade would be optional, for those students who wished to continue their studies in the Hebrew program; for most students, however, the seventh grade would be reserved for bar or bat mitzvah instruction plus religious school. The board of the central agency approved the plan and suggested that it be presented to the three congregations.

The executive director obtained the support of all the rabbis and then brought the restructuring plan to the religious education committees of the three congregations. One congregation sent a survey to the families affected by the change, in order to elicit a better understanding of its congregants' attitude toward the issue. The other congregations made a decision either in committee or in a conference of the rabbi and the chairperson of the religious education committee. In these two congregations, parents at large were not consulted, nor were most of them aware of the changes being sought.

In the spring of the year, the three congregations ratified the restructuring, and all parents were informed of the change. Shortly afterward a groundswell of negative reaction emerged from a number of parents, threatening to undermine the entire project. Congregants, angry about what they perceived as an imposed change, held private meetings. A group of parents called a meeting to which the executive director and the president of the central agency were invited. At this meeting they brought up issues beyond the one of beginning Hebrew school in the third grade.

The parents complained that the school dictated policies without requesting their advice or taking into account their feelings, and they were "fed up."

See pages 88–89 for General Questions for All Case Vignettes and for The Guiding Principles of Leadership Practices.

Additional Discussion Questions for This Case

1. To what extent were the costs and options associated with a centralized plan to teach Hebrew versus those associated with a decentralized plan fully documented and shared with those affected?
2. If all parents had been consulted, would there have been less resistance to the plan?
3. What role should parents play in shaping a school's short-term and long-term goals?
4. In the course of planning changes, how can a school "take the pulse" of its constituencies?
5. How would a long-range planning process have helped in this situation?

Suggested Options

1. It may be best to put the changes on hold and engage in a more sophisticated long-range planning process that would involve all constituencies (parents, educators, rabbis, and lay leaders of the congregations) in defining the problems and choosing the solutions.
2. Convene separate focus groups of parents, students, and teachers to explain the plan and to discuss perceptions of the school's goals, its problems, and participants' reactions to the

new plan. Based on the results of these meetings, the plan could be continued, discarded, or modified.

3. Implement the changes in the seventh grade, and mount a public relations effort to begin the midweek classes in the third grade.

Managing Change

Case 9 ▾ Change Can Be User-Friendly*

Linda Shapiro has come up through the ranks from Hebrew school teacher in a small suburban congregational school to her current position as an experienced administrator in a large suburban congregational school. When Ms. Shapiro took over her position, her staff consisted of twenty teachers, all of whom had been in the school a long time. During her initial observations of, and conversations with, the teachers, it emerged that some of them had problems with classroom management and that their teaching skills varied widely. It was also clear that the curriculum needed to be changed. Ms. Shapiro recalls that

at the first meeting the teachers said, "You're not going to start making changes, are you?" It was obvious that they were terrified of change, so I didn't do anything right away, but I started looking for things that could support the changes I wanted to make. I saw that most students attend school three days a week and that each day has three time slots: the program is totally departmentalized. Thus, depending on the subject and the need, some classes can be very small and some large. Now the teachers who have difficulty with classroom management have small classes, and those who like that kind of challenge have the large ones.

---

* This vignette can also be used to illustrate the skill area of Managing Staff.

Ms. Shapiro realized that a major scheduling issue could become part of the solution to another of her problems:

> Students attended school three days a week, (Shabbat plus two weekdays,) but they were scheduled on alternate days. For example, midweek days for a *gimel* class could be Monday and Wednesday or Tuesday and Thursday. This was a nightmare for assigning teachers. So, despite some parental opposition, the school board established a fixed schedule, so that multiple sections of the same grade met at the same time. Now that teachers were teaching the same grade at the same time, they could team-teach. I could schedule less experienced teachers with strong ones. I never said they had to team-teach; I just discussed the idea and let it happen. Now I'm ready to tackle the curriculum.

See pages 88–89 for General Questions for All Case Vignettes and for The Guiding Principles of Leadership Principles.

Additional Discussion Questions for This Case

1. What role should the faculty play in setting priorities for the school and in solving its problems?
2. To what extent did the administrator explore the teachers' concerns about changes?
3. What is your assessment of her solutions?

Managing Change

Case 10 ▾ Growth Can Mean Upheaval*

Harold Marks, a product of the Brandeis Education Program, has been educational director of a large metropolitan synagogue for twelve years. The synagogue's religious school students live in surrounding neighborhoods as well as in more distant suburbs. During Mr. Marks' tenure the synagogue has experienced a renewal, and the school population has grown about 10 percent a year. Eventually it was decided to construct a new building to accommodate the growth.

For a year Mr. Marks learned what it was like to manage a dispersed organization. Classes met in three different public schools in the suburbs, in a different building every day of the week. The congregation had to pay the costs of rent and transportation. Some children who lived very far away were privately tutored for the year; although the school did not provide the tutors, it did provide the parents with a list of names.

The challenge of coordinating the program was immense. There was no office except a trailer on the construction site, no phone by which to reach the schools, no library, no supply room, and no book room. Teachers had to do their preparation and planning independently of the school, the central office, and one another. Parents were less involved than before because there was no place for them to congregate during school hours.

There were some positive aspects to the situation, however. The school acquired a mobile van and twenty-five cases of supplies. Mr. Marks acquired a cellular phone and learned to use a

---

* This vignette can also be used to illustrate the skill areas of Managing Staff and Managing Space.

trailer as his main office. He found that everything went all right once it was organized and that he liked being free of some administrative duties:

> I got to do more classroom observation and was closer to teachers and students than ever before. In emergencies I even did some teaching. Most teachers responded to the challenge by overlooking small problems and banding together to deal with the situation—in some ways morale was better than usual. And parents were supportive and understanding too. It should have been an awful year, but it wasn't. I don't know why.

See pages 88–89 for General Questions for All Case Vignettes and for The Guiding Principles of Leadership Practices.

Additional Discussion Questions for This Case

1. Why wasn't this "an awful year"?
2. What lessons can Mr. Marks learn from the experience that can help him improve the school even after they move into the new building?
3. How might the circumstances have been different in a small community? How might they have been different with a different population?

Managing Change

Case 11 ▼ Solving That Age-Old Bar and Bat Mitzvah Problem*

Overall David Schwartz feels he has done a good job as educational director of his large Conservative congregation. As supervisor of the program from nursery school through eighth grade and as a participant in the governance of a community high school, he has generally presided over growth and built a strong, cohesive program with a core of experienced and dependable teachers.

Nonetheless, he decided he had to mobilize staff members to confront an "age-old problem" in the school: what to do with post-bar and bat mitzvah eighth graders. The structure of the religious school is such that after the eighth grade, students enter the community high school. Most eighth graders are post-bar or bat mitzvah, although a few become bar or bat mitzvah during that year. There was nothing "special" about the eighth grade, and teachers agreed that for the most part it was a "holding action until graduation." Mr. Schwartz believed the problem was more than a question of the students' being bored: "It was a community norm for students to graduate from eighth grade, but the retention rate in the high school was down to 40 percent. I believed that the disaffection that began in eighth grade was influencing students to drop out later."

He called together the teachers from the seventh and eighth grades and presented his views on the problem. He says, "I didn't present any solutions because I wasn't sure what to do." The teachers believed that any decisions regarding a revision of the

---

* This vignette can also be used to illustrate the skill areas of Managing Staff and Relating to Parents and Students.

eighth grade curriculum must be made in consultation with the other teachers in the school so that they could jointly create a "wish list of what eighth graders should come away from this school with." The members of the faculty grouped themselves according to the subjects they taught and put together a course of study that included not only the eighth grade but a modified plan for the whole school. Mr. Schwartz reports that "the initial results are promising, and there's increased enthusiasm in the eighth grade among students. The most important change, though, is in the teachers. This was the first time in recent years that they have been called upon to do some real creating—it's really recharged them."

See pages 88–89 for General Questions for All Case Vignettes and for The Guiding Principles of Leadership Practices.

Additional Discussion Questions for This Case

1. What other groups might have been consulted about solving the problem but were not?
2. What principles of institutional change were included in Mr. Schwartz's approach?

Managing Change

Case 12 ▾ The Stresses of Managing Change*

The day school in a distant suburb of a large city grew from a relatively small operation to one that could no longer be adequately coordinated by a single full-time principal. The principal, a Jewish educator, had hired a general studies coordinator several years earlier but now was finding that he must pay more attention to the Jewish studies curriculum as well. As the student body had grown increasingly diverse in recent years, more students now had special needs, and classes were getting so large that addressing individual needs was becoming more difficult. Furthermore, as the faculty got larger and busier, the informal channels of communication about curriculum were no longer sufficient to ensure a smooth transition from grade to grade. Finally, the principal was becoming increasingly busy with the daily operation of the school, with parents' meetings, with fund-raising, and with recruitment.

Dr. Jesse Baum, the principal, convinced the school board that it was necessary to create the position of curriculum coordinator for the Hebrew program for the second through sixth grades. The board agreed to a part-time curriculum coordinator and authorized Dr. Baum to select a person to fill the position.

For several reasons Dr. Baum decided to choose someone from the school faculty. For one thing, he was aware of the difficulty of finding experienced administrators or coordinators to work part-time. In addition, he believed it was important to create opportunities for advancement among the faculty. As a professional educator he always tried to keep up with the journals on educational

---

* This vignette can also be used to illustrate the skill areas of Managing Staff and Managing Day-to-Day Operations.

research, and he was well aware of the research on teacher professionalism and satisfaction, which indicated that it was important for teachers to have opportunities to grow and develop professionally and to acquire and use new professional skills. Thus, he chose one of the school's veteran Hebrew teachers, offering her a reduced teaching load and added compensation in exchange for the added responsibilities of the part-time curriculum coordinator. The teacher accepted the position.

The new position was clearly defined as curriculum coordinator. The coordinator's role would be to work with the teachers to plan and implement changes in the curriculum. She would also design and moderate staff development sessions around these changes. Although the members of the Jewish studies faculty were fully informed of the teacher's responsibilities and knew that they included no supervisory or evaluative component, the faculty members resisted the change. Many met the promotion with jealousy and resentment, and several refused to comply with the coordinator's requests. Not only was the curriculum work not getting done, but staff morale was becoming a greater issue than ever before.

Dr. Baum realized that he may have created more problems than he resolved, and he knew he had to find a solution to the situation.

See pages 88–89 for General Questions for All Case Vignettes and for The Guiding Principles of Leadership Practices.

Additional Discussion Questions for This Case

1. How would life have been different for Dr. Baum if he had first approached his faculty members with the issue of curriculum coordinator and requested their ideas and suggestions?

2. What preparation should the new coordinator have received in advance of the promotion?

3. To what extent might faculty resistance have been related to the lack of specification about who would pick up the half-time teaching load dropped by the new coordinator? ·

4. How can you create a career ladder within a school without causing resentment and jealousy?

Managing Lay-Professional Relations

Case 13 ▾ It's Not Easy to Tell Who Is in Charge*

Joan Liebowitz began her first administrative experience with a complex set of responsibilities. She had to design a curriculum, recruit and train teachers, and learn to cope with a lay board and the rabbi, all of whom, it seemed to her, were in charge of the school. "I do the hiring and the firing," she said, "so there's no role for the school board there. But the school board does the budget, makes personnel policies, decides on benefits, and sets salaries. They always seem to be worried about the school needing too much, but they don't really know what the school needs as much as I do."

The rabbi sometimes attends the meetings of the school board. Ms. Liebowitz observes,

> He cares about quality education, but he is too busy to do much about it, and he is not a professional educator anyway. I thought it made good sense at first to meet with the rabbi regularly, to make sure that our views on education were in agreement and that information was shared. But we gradually stopped meeting, and I think that's fine with him.
>
> Actually, I thought I was doing fine with the school board until the first complaint came up. Seventeen families complained about a classroom-management problem, and the board said to me, "It's your job to handle those

---

* This vignette can also be used to illustrate the skill area of Defining Roles.

things. What are you doing there anyway?" So from that I learned to document everything I do.

My first two years I met with the school board chair on a weekly basis. At the synagogue board meeting the chair reported on the activities of the school, and I was only there as an observer. I was thrilled when the president appointed a new school board chair who is a professional educator. But weeks went by, and I didn't hear from her. After several months she came to visit me, and I told her that I was disappointed in her lack of support and interest. She pointed out that the phone works both ways; she was leaving it up to me to take charge of the school and notify her when I needed help. Sometimes it seems like everybody is in charge here and sometimes like nobody is.

See pages 88–89 for General Questions for All Case Vignettes and for The Guiding Principles of Leadership Practices.

Additional Discussion Questions for This Case

1. Who has the primary relationship-building responsibilities in the lay-professional relationship?
2. What could the principal do to make better use of the rabbi's supervisory relationships?

Suggested Options

1. Work harder at maintaining relationships with the rabbi and the school chairperson. Meet as frequently with each as appropriate to keep the lines of communication open. Since she seems to have some problems with communication, Ms. Liebowitz should begin by reflecting on what she hopes to

discuss (perhaps role-playing with her colleagues in the beginning). Before making any key decisions, she should send memos to both the rabbi and the school chairperson, asking for advice and input.

2. Develop a clearer job description for the educational director by conferring with all the key players. To assist in this process, keep a log documenting tasks and time. It may be useful to suggest a school board retreat to address the issue of role definition.

3. Bring in a consultant to assess and analyze the problems of school governance, role definition, and lay-professional relations.

Managing Lay-Professional Relations

Case 14 ▼ Critical Benefits

Wilma Lasky was the full-time educational director and family-life coordinator for the supplementary school of a congregation located in a wealthy suburb of New York City. She was the only full-time wage earner in her family; her husband was a part-time student and a part-time teacher and tutor. Ms. Lasky was paying four thousand dollars a year for medical insurance with a five-hundred-dollar deductible for herself and another five-hundred-dollar deductible for her husband. She said, "I desperately need a good medical plan; this one is not only expensive but inadequate. The maternity benefits are so bad that we can't even consider starting a family."

Contract negotiations for Ms. Lasky's position were about to begin, and she was determined to "go to the mat with this issue." The board members' position was that if they offer benefits to one person, they will have to offer them "to everyone," although only three full-time professionals appeared to be eligible. Ms. Lasky said, "This is a serious problem for people in my position. Jewish educators are not treated as professionally as other professionals; so this is an issue of principle as well as need."

See pages 88–89 for General Questions for All Case Vignettes and for The Guiding Principles of Leadership Practices.

Additional Discussion Questions for This Case

1. Is there evidence that Jewish organizations single out Jewish educators by not treating them as professionals? What evidence suggests that this is not necessarily true?

2. What can small organizations do to provide fringe benefits to staff members in ways that are efficient and effective?

3. Is it to Mr. Lasky's advantage to treat this as a matter of principle? In her discussions with the board, should she articulate it as such, or as a simpler compensation issue? Why?

Managing Lay-Professional Relations

Case 15 ▾ Lay-Professional Relations in a Day School*

Rabbi Abrams is the director of a large K–12 Orthodox day school in a major metropolitan area. Officially it is a community school, and it receives substantial support from the federation of Jewish agencies. Rabbi Abrams places a great deal of emphasis on teaching, developing interpersonal relationships with students and families outside the classroom, and fostering a religious community. The school has been very successful and has received national awards for achievement, and Rabbi Abrams enjoys considerable popularity in the community.

The rabbi has been less successful in other areas. He has been unable to create the kind of board that can strengthen the school's viability, and he has been unable to develop relationships with the board members, who are generally parents whose critical concerns regarding their own children have prompted them to volunteer to serve. He finds it hard to attract strong community leaders who can provide either financial support for the school or support for his vision of the rabbi's role. If such congregants do sit on the board, they tend to leave it quickly to serve communal organizations such as the federation. As a result, board members tend to "think small" and parochially.

For example, the board members tend to define the role of the rabbi very narrowly. The previous president expressed strong concerns about the time that Rabbi Abrams spends doing outreach work in the community. The president wanted the rabbi to be more visible in the school and less visible in the community, and

---

* This vignette can also be used to illustrate the skill area of Defining Roles.

he wrote an item into the rabbi's contract, stipulating the percentage of time he must allocate to different tasks. Rabbi Abrams objected strongly to this, and the board eliminated it from the final version of the contract. Nonetheless, the rabbi anticipates new problems of the same type in his next salary negotiation. He also worries because he is now in a salary range that exceeds that of most of the board members. He fears that in negotiations this fact alone may evoke negative feelings and result in unpalatable contract conditions.

See pages 88–89 for General Questions for All Case Vignettes and for The Guiding Principles of Leadership Practices.

Additional Discussion Questions for This Case

1. How should the board conduct the rabbi's annual performance review?
2. What role should the rabbi play in designing the school director's job description?
3. What could the rabbi do to alter the composition of the board?
4. How can one train laypersons to pay more attention to process and less attention to relationships?

Managing Lay-Professional Relations

Case 16 ▼ Starting a New School*

In the late 1970s leaders of four congregations in a suburb of a major metropolitan city with a large Jewish population decided to join forces and start a one-day-a-week innovative high school of Jewish studies. They invited Phyllis Levine, a woman about fifty years of age, to be the first principal. Ms. Levine had become a Jewish educator after a career change several years earlier, and this was her first administrative experience. It was a part-time job (with very part-time pay), but she went at it with remarkable vigor and enthusiasm. Her role was complex. She had to design the curriculum, recruit and hire teachers, recruit students, work with a lay board and rabbis as well as with the boards of the individual synagogues, work with parents, and plan informal activities.

The board's goal was to open the school with 100 students, but Ms. Levine secretly believed they would be lucky to have 80. The school actually opened with more than 130 students, although in subsequent years the number stabilized between 100 and 110. The school was organized with three Sunday morning classes, including a core curriculum and a choice of electives.

The school began with a provisional board, some of whose members continued to serve after the board was officially established. The official board consisted of the rabbis of the four congregations, two representatives from each congregation and its religious school, and a representative of the local central agency. The first year the board met monthly to set the agenda for the

---

* This vignette can also be used to illustrate the skill areas of Managing Change and Managing Oneself.

school. Later there were fewer meetings. The board was supportive of Ms. Levine and eager to let her "take the school and run with it." At first the board members didn't see themselves as watchdogs and were positive about what they saw as her vision.

Ms. Levine recalled that her work with the school "was the most exciting and positive professional experience" she'd ever had. During the first years she did "everything," and the school and its reputation flourished, although it needed more financial support. She wanted more retreats and more creative programming. She wanted to expand the board so that it would include more influential laypersons. She recruited the outgoing president of one congregation, of which she was a member, and, she said, "He became active all right, but he turned out to be a political animal who wanted to build his own power at the expense of mine." He objected to some of her requests, including her next raise in pay. He persuaded the board to offer her half her requested salary increase because, he told her, "if we give you what you ask, we will have to offer the same percentage increase to all synagogue personnel." The board also offered her a two-year contract, although her previous contract had been for three years. After five years in the school, she decided she would not accept the terms, and she resigned.

See pages 88–89 for General Questions for All Case Vignettes and for The Guiding Principles of Leadership Practices.

Additional Discussion Questions for This Case

1. To what extent did the principal select the wrong board members?
2. What is the professional's role in building the board?

3. Could the principal have done more to assess the new member's concerns once he was on the board?
4. How could other board members have been involved in the situation?
5. Should a board of directors be a "watchdog"?
6. What should a board of directors of a school do? How should it be organized?

Managing Staff

Case 17 ▾ A Teacher's Resistance to Change[*]

Eli Cohen is educational director of a large and well-established congregational school in a major city. The school has a faculty of twenty-two teachers, about half of whom have been teaching there for eight years or more. Although the school continues to have a good reputation, the quality of instruction and classroom management has been uneven in the last few years, and there has been a series of complaints from parents. Furthermore, enrollment in the religious school has been declining.

Mr. Cohen was hired for the position three years ago with the mandate of improving the school and its image. His goal during his three-year contract period has been to promote innovative teaching and engage students in the learning process. He claims that he chose to achieve this goal in part by making his presence felt in the classroom and demonstrating to teachers that he cared about education and was not just an administrator. He instituted a process of regular classroom observation, a practice that had been rarely carried out by his predecessor.

Mr. Cohen observed Shira Stern's class twice. Although she appeared to be well prepared each time, the lessons did not go smoothly. He noted that she was especially creative with the use of teaching materials and visual aids and that she probably spent many hours in preparation. Nonetheless, she was tense and ill at ease with the children. She concentrated on covering material and mastering content, but she rarely smiled or gave a compliment. During his observation, Mr. Cohen reminded himself that

---

[*] This vignette can also be used to illustrate the skill area of Managing Change.

he had heard Ms. Stern say to others that she prides herself on keeping control in the classroom.

Mr. Cohen spoke to Ms. Stern about her manner and affect in the classroom. She immediately became defensive and claimed that his presence made her nervous. She was not used to being "supervised" or observed.

Ms. Stern is one of the veteran teachers in the school, and she exerts a great deal of influence on her fellow staff members. One of the newer teachers told Mr. Cohen in confidence that Ms. Stern was stirring up bad feelings about him, claiming he was picking on her and finding fault with her because he was not capable of assisting teachers with instruction or classroom management. She was even considering complaining to the chairperson of the school board and to the rabbi, and she was trying to muster support from others so she could "represent the staff."

Coincidentally, as this was happening and as Mr. Cohen was considering both the feedback he would give Ms. Stern on the second classroom observation and the evaluation he must write, the president recommended Ms. Stern to him as the faculty representative to the board of directors.

See pages 88–89 for General Questions for All Case Vignettes and for The Guiding Principles of Leadership Practices.

Additional Discussion Questions for This Case

1. What should the principal say to the president of the board about faculty representation?
2. If it is true that the principal does not know how to assist a veteran teacher, what might he do?
3. How does one effect change in a school?
4. How does one create a climate that promotes growth and change in a staff? Can such change be imposed from above?

Suggested Options

1. Have a discussion with the entire staff on supervisory practices and what makes the teachers feel comfortable. Emphasize that supervision involves looking at both strengths and weaknesses, and consider a clinical-supervision approach, in which the teacher chooses the aspect of the lesson that is to be the focus of classroom observation, thereby allowing the teacher to experience some control over the situation. Follow up this discussion with a post-observation conference on the agreed-upon focus, and then consider a tactful and more general discussion of educational issues and practices.

2. Mr. Cohen should talk to the president of the congregation about procedures for appointing a faculty representative to the board. The educational director and/or the faculty as a whole should have some say in the matter.

3. At a meeting with Ms. Stern, Mr. Cohen could ask her to share her concerns with him. This should not occur at the same time as her observation conference. Mr. Cohen should emphasize the positive, recognizing Ms. Stern's strong background in teaching and valued years in the congregational school, and he should discuss ways in which they could work together. He should respond fairly but firmly, however, with regard to what is unacceptable and unprofessional behavior. As the relationship improves, he could also suggest workshops that explore some of the affective techniques that make for a more relaxed classroom.

Managing Staff

Case 18 ▼ Firing a Teacher

When at the age of thirty Dan Gordon became the educational director of a large Conservative congregation in the Midwest, there were more than four hundred children in the religious school. One of his responsibilities was supervising the educational program from nursery school through the eighth grade, which included a leading role in the hiring and firing of teachers.

Six of the teachers were members of the congregation, with long-standing relationships within the synagogue. This was not generally a problem, but in his second year Mr. Gordon found it necessary to dismiss one of these teachers, who was also the daughter of a past president of the congregation. He described the situation:

She was experiencing serious emotional problems following separation from her husband, taking it out on her kids in the classroom. When kids acted out or misbehaved in the classroom, she yelled and screamed, saying things like "If I needed someone to talk back to me, I would go back home to my husband." Parents complained about the way she was treating their children. I tried talking to her, but she was in no shape to deal with the problem. When I finally suggested that she leave, she created a stir in the community, blaming the whole situation on me. I subsequently initiated discussions with the school board chair, president, and the rabbi, and she was let go in the middle of the year, but the talk about my role in dismissing her continued for quite a while and caused quite a bit of divisiveness in the congregation.

See pages 88–89 for General Questions for All Case Vignettes and for The Guiding Principles of Leadership Practices.

Additional Discussion Questions for This Case

1. What could the principal have done to avert the crisis? Did he wait too long to initiate discussions with the rabbi and lay leaders, or was his behavior appropriate?
2. Is it appropriate for members of a congregation to be paid teachers in the congregation's religious school? What are the advantages and disadvantages of such an arrangement?

Managing Staff

Case 19 ▾ When a Teacher Doesn't Fit

Ellen Marcus was the first full-time principal of a K–6 day school in a fairly large city. The school had opened with just a kindergarten and first grade and then had added a grade each year. During the early years of the school, one of its most distinguishing features was its warm, family atmosphere. Because of its small size and pioneering spirit, there was a sense of community among the teachers, children, and parents.

Mrs. Marcus came to the school in its fifth year, when the enrollment had reached 135. It was no longer a tiny school. Since new classes were being added each year, one of Mrs. Marcus' major efforts was hiring new staff members and assisting them in adjusting to the culture and mission of the school. Because the school was located near both a major university with a strong Judaica department and a college of Jewish studies, Mrs. Marcus often recruited teachers who were graduating from those institutions.

One such person was Gail Simon, who was hired to teach the first grade Hebrew class. Ms. Simon carefully planned and prepared for the class, but after her first classroom observation Mrs. Marcus had some concerns about the teacher's manner: she lacked the special spark and enthusiasm that Mrs. Marcus had hoped to see. Her lack of warmth was disturbing to Mrs. Marcus, to parents, and even to the chairperson of the education committee, who considered Ms. Simon to be a "cold fish" and not sufficiently loving or giving for a first grade classroom.

During evaluation sessions Mrs. Marcus found that Ms. Simon seemed hurt and became withdrawn whenever the issue of her classroom manner was raised. Nonetheless, despite Mrs. Marcus' concern that Ms. Simon might never become the type of teacher she envisioned for the school, she rehired her for a second year, assigning her to a fourth grade, where her lack of warmth might not be as important. Her teaching in that grade was adequate but ordinary. She maintained good control of the class but evinced no spark or excitement, and the children responded in kind.

During evaluation sessions Ms. Simon was defensive, stating that she knew Mrs. Marcus didn't like her. Mrs. Marcus found it hard to dissuade her because the principal's criticisms mostly concerned the teacher's personality. She finally decided not to rehire her because although she is an "adequate teacher, she just didn't fit." But Mrs. Marcus had yet to decide how she would present the decision to Ms. Simon.

See pages 88–89 for General Questions for All Case Vignettes and for The Guiding Principles of Leadership Practices.

Additional Discussion Questions for This Case

1. How well did the principal document the teacher's performance?
2. To what extent could a third party be used to assess adequacy of "fit"?
3. What qualities do you look for in a teacher?
4. How do you present bad news to a person?
5. To what extent can a supervisor really effect change in a teacher?

Managing Staff

Case 20 ▼ A Master Teacher, A Difficult Person

Jay Sugarman is the principal of a supplementary school in a large urban congregation. Despite his twelve years of experience in this school and five years' previous experience as an administrator, he has been finding it very difficult to work with one of his most experienced and most talented teachers. He termed her "a master teacher in the classroom," but outside of the classroom, he said, she is "a terror." According to Mr. Sugarman, "No contract ever satisfies her; she constantly seeks exceptions to the terms of her contract and questions all aspects of the conditions of employment, from her hours to the parking available." Furthermore, she fomented dissatisfaction among a group of teachers for whom she is a leader. The result was a lowering of morale and a need for Mr. Sugarman to "put out brushfires" among the staff all the time. In addition, this teacher is active in the congregation and has stirred up issues concerning the school at every opportunity.

Mr. Sugarman tried talking to the teacher many times—kindly, sternly, angrily—but to no avail. He also tried steering her toward additional part-time teaching and tutoring opportunities to assuage her complaint about not earning enough money. This, too, failed to satisfy her "crusade to cause trouble." Nonetheless, her performance in the classroom remains unmatched among the staff; in addition to her superb teaching, she is dependable, always prepared, and extremely knowledgeable. Mr. Sugarman wondered, "Is it worth it to have the best teacher in the world if her behavior outside the classroom is keeping you awake at night. And if I fire her, will she cause trouble in the congregation anyway, so I'll have lost a teacher and still not gained peace of mind?"

See pages 88–89 for General Questions for All Case Vignettes and for The Guiding Principles of Leadership Practices.

Additional Discussion Questions for This Case

1. To what extent are principals paid to manage the complaints of staff members, even if the complaints are unrelenting?
2. To what extent can the rabbi be a resource in this situation?
3. Might the teacher have a hidden agenda?

Managing Staff

Case 21 ▾ The Never-Ending Saga of Recruitment

For Ben Frankel, as it is for many supplementary administrators, every year the recruiting of a teaching staff is the tough story of always solving the last problem at the last minute—if at all:

> I've been doing this job for ten years, and I've had at least that many philosophies about hiring staff. At first I used to recruit students from a nearby university. I signed contracts with them, but they didn't honor them. For example, they were supposed to honor our calendar, and instead they stayed on their calendar, and they were gone during university breaks.
>
> Then I changed the policy. I tried recruiting through referrals. I tried to recruit retired professionals. I tried an avocational program. Finally I got very aggressive in my outreach to the community, buttonholing people that I met at meetings or social events who might be appropriate and canvassing every group I met with or spoke to. If I wasn't fully staffed for the following year by the end of June, I prayed for things like an Israeli family traveling from New York to L.A. losing their way and ending up in our city. In truth, the best I could hope for was the transfer of an employee to our area with a spouse who could teach Hebrew school.

For a while the synagogue offered free membership as an inducement to teachers. Then that was reduced to free tickets for the High Holidays. Mr. Frankel remarks, "Some people think that offering benefits is like bribing people to teach. I don't see it that way."

See pages 88–89 for General Questions for All Case Vignettes and for The Guiding Principles of Leadership Practices.

Additional Discussion Questions for This Case

1. What kind of annual recruitment plan could the administrator develop?
2. How should he involve the synagogue board in identifying incentives?
3. What could Mr. Frankel do to improve retention of his staff so that he wouldn't have to expend so much energy on recruitment?

Managing Staff

Case 22 ▾ Painless Teacher Observation

Aaron Wise became the administrator of a supplementary school when he was young and most of the teachers on his staff were old enough to be his mother. He described the experience:

They didn't let me forget it, especially when I went to observe their classes. One older teacher told me that she didn't think there was anything I could tell her about teaching that she didn't already know, and I agreed. But I told her that I would like to be like an extra pair of eyes, sort of a video camera in her room. . . . So after I watched her class, I pointed out some of the behaviors of certain children and asked if she was aware of them. She was pleased about that and said that she was so happy that I hadn't used a structured observation instrument, which she seemed to fear.

I figured if that was true of her, it was probably true of other teachers as well. So I developed informal observation into a system. First I gave teachers a choice—I could observe one full class or come in and out during the course of a week. Then instead of a form I wrote copious notes in the classroom and discussed what I had written with the teacher soon after I completed the observation form. We didn't always agree on what I'd seen or how I interpreted it. So we would argue, and I would see the teacher's perspective as often as I could. The final step in my observation system is to write a one- or two-page letter documenting my observations—this letter always has as many positives as I can honestly put in it, and I made sure that my criticism is as constructive as I can make it.

See pages 88–89 for General Questions for All Case Vignettes and for The Guiding Principles of Leadership Practices.

Additional Discussion Questions for This Case

1. What alternative kinds of supervisory techniques are available to educators—for example, peer supervision, differentiated supervision, and so forth?
2. How did good listening skills benefit Mr. Wise?
3. Can supervision be made less threatening?

Managing Staff

Case 23 ▼ Supporting Your Teachers*

Miriam Handler felt very honored when after eleven years of teaching in a K–6 day school, she was asked to be the school's principal. At that time the school had about 250 children and a faculty of twenty-four full- and part-time teachers. Based on her twenty years of teaching experience, Ms. Handler made the resolution that she would support her teachers in their dealings with both parents and children. She said, "Too many times I had seen teachers told to solve a problem themselves or even leave it unsolved, just so nobody would make waves with the parents. I didn't know if I could agree with every teacher every time, but I was sure I could make them know they were supported."

Ms. Handler's challenge came in the spring of her first year as an administrator, when both the Hebrew teacher and the general studies teacher of a third grade class requested a meeting with her to discuss a child in their class who presented a persistent behavior problem:

They came in my room all wound up and ready to ventilate. So I sat down with them and asked them to speak, first presenting "good news" and then "bad news." The teachers said that the child is bright and capable and does quite well on tests "when he studies." But the bad news included constant lateness, failure to bring in homework, disrespect to teachers, and a disregard of the punishments they employed with him.

Then I asked the teachers about other steps they had

---

* This vignette can also be used to illustrate the skill area of Managing Day-to-Day Oprations.

taken. They responded that they had sent a note home to the parents, who had signed it but not otherwise responded. I made suggestions about ways they might speak to the child and said I thought a phone call to the parents, explaining the whole situation might be helpful. Finally I said we would regroup in a week and talk again and perhaps call the parent in for a discussion if we felt it was warranted. Later I heard that the child was behaving much better, "because of the principal's intervention." Of course, all I did was support the teachers and make them feel efficacious—they did the rest.

See pages 88–89 for General Questions for All Case Vignettes and for The Guiding Principles of Leadership Practices.

Additional Discussion Questions for This Case

1. What might the principal have done if the situation had deteriorated rather than improved?
2. How can the principal determine whether the problem is the child or the teachers' insufficient instructional skills?
3. What were the teachers' and the principal's hidden agendas here?

Managing Staff

Case 24 ▼ Why Can't Parents Help?

Most of the families and staff members in this small city congregational school of 150 students know each other well, both
inside and outside the synagogue, as it is a relatively tight knit
community. Either because of or in spite of this, disruptive behavior in the Hebrew school can be a serious problem, especially
when students reach the *heh* class (equivalent to the seventh grade
in secular school).

Behavior was particularly bad in this year's *heh* class. Of the
twenty students, a clique of five boys created such severe disrup-
tion that the educational program for the entire class could not
proceed. The three teachers working with that grade could no
longer manage the class and asked to meet with the educational
director. After the meeting they decided on a plan. First the
teachers called in the parents of the five students for a friendly
"let's work this out" talk. Not much happened, but the parents
agreed to move on to step two: the school called a meeting of the
five students, their parents, the teachers, the educational director,
and the rabbi to talk about the nature of the problem and to elicit
helpful suggestions. The parents were not hostile, but they were
not helpful either, and it became clear that the behavior problems
did not occur only in Hebrew school.

The staff met again with the educational director and decided
to call a general meeting of all the *heh* class parents and to invite a
psychologist to discuss adolescence and its problems. As a result of
that program, a "positive reward system" was implemented for all
students in the *heh* class. Teachers felt somewhat better about the
situation, but some parents were not happy about what had transpired, and it was learned that they had called a "secret meeting"

to discuss their suspicions about the school's inability to deal with the children. Part of the problem was resolved when some of the disruptive students stopped coming to Hebrew school after they became b'nai mitzvah.

Later that year some parents met with the school board to make suggestions for the eighth grade class, but the effort never gained momentum and faded out.

See pages 88–89 for General Questions for All Case Vignettes and for The Guiding Principles of Leadership Practice.

Additional Discussion Questions for This Case

1. How should a school go about making parents partners in the education process?
2. What is the appropriate role of parents in a congregational school?
3. How is this different from the role of parents in a day school?

Relating to Parents and Students

Case 25 ▼ Disruptive Parents

As headmaster of a small but growing and educationally excellent day school, Alex Green prided himself on his accessibility to parents. He began his relationship with each student's parents by participating in a pre-enrollment interview. As was his practice, he met with Deborah's parents, an older couple who had no other children. At his first meeting with them, they bragged profusely about their daughter's intelligence and emphasized her need for a very special school to challenge her sufficiently. They insisted that if she were not kept busy, she would be bored, and she really needed a heavy dose of academics. Mr. Green was a bit uneasy about the conversation because the assessment test administered by the school psychologist indicated that Deborah was just about average in intelligence and readiness.

After school began, Deborah's parents came to Mr. Green's office regularly, almost weekly, with one complaint or another. They typically implied that the school and the teacher were not challenging Deborah sufficiently, but when Mr. Green checked with Deborah's teachers and when he observed her behavior in the classroom, he found the opposite to be true. Actually, Deborah often had trouble attending to the task at hand and was behind the class in most areas. She also seemed to be under a great deal of pressure and was not getting along well with the other children. When Mr. Green shared this information with Deborah's parents, they became angry and accused him and the teacher of not doing their jobs. They said they would bring the issue before the education committee. A few weeks later the teacher began to suspect that Deborah may have a learning disability, and he wanted Mr. Green to take some action.

See pages 88–89 for General Questions for All Case Vignettes and for The Guiding Principles of Leadership Practices.

Additional Discussion Questions for This Case

1. What might the headmaster have done to focus earlier on the discrepancy between the child's performance and the parents' expectations?
2. Did Mr. Green involve the teacher in the process sufficiently?
3. What support services need to be available in order to do a proper job in a day school?

Suggested Options

1. A team approach should be used to assess and address the problem. The team should include the school psychologist, the student's teachers, and Mr. Green. The team members could work together to discover what approaches and materials work best with Deborah. Following a staff meeting, the parents should be invited for a meeting with the team, at which each teacher working with the child would point out the girl's strengths and weaknesses and describe what was being done to meet Deborah's needs. The team would then invite the parents to offer feedback and voice their concerns. The team members and the parents should agree on a plan of action, set target dates for further review, and set up a system for maintaining regular phone contact. After laying the groundwork with this procedure, further evaluation and testing may be suggested.

2. It is possible that the rational procedures will not work. The administration may decide that the school's program is beyond Deborah's capabilities and that her presence should be allowed only in conjunction with family counseling and appropriate tutoring.

3. A problem-solving process should be established whereby students' parents speak first with the teachers and then with the administrator. The education committee should make clear that parents should bring an issue to the committee only under extreme circumstances and that issues of an individual student's education should be handled by the professional staff.

Relating to Parents and Students

Case 26 ▾ The Disruptive Student*

Dina Lewis is the educational director of a congregational school of about one hundred students in a small community. She is a veteran administrator who is soon to retire, and on the whole she remembers her career as a fulfilling one. She relates a recent problem:

I have enjoyed being a Jewish educator, but I have recently had one of the most frustrating experiences of my career. It concerns a very disruptive student—one that neither the teachers nor I could handle during the three years he has been in the school. His brother and sister are also troublesome, but he is really uncontrollable. He annoys the other students; he takes things from them; he is abusive to the teachers. And his parents have repeatedly refused to acknowledge his unacceptable behavior. Instead, they blame everyone and everything, from staff to other kids to any circumstances.

The temple has a long-established policy for handling disruptive students, with a detailed, step-by-step procedure. The first step involves trying to get the teacher to handle the situation. Most of the time the teacher resolves it with the child and the parents. A next step is for me to get involved, and it may require a parent conference with the teacher, the parents, and myself.

A final and rare step is suspension, which is a really

---

* This vignette can aslo be used to illustrate the skill area of Managing Lay-Professional Relations.

difficult decision to make since we don't like to deny a Jewish education to any child. In the case of this student, we went to the final step, which involved a meeting with the family, the rabbi, the congregational president, and me. At this meeting the parents threatened to resign from the congregation and hinted strongly that legal action would be taken against the staff if the child was suspended. Although before the meeting the president had agreed with our decision to suspend the child, in the face of these threats he backed down, and the student continued to attend school. Now even seasoned teachers don't want this child or any of his family in their classes, and in addition the teachers and I feel betrayed by the president.

See pages 88–89 for General Questions for All Case Vignettes and for The Guiding Principles of Leadership Practices.

Additional Discussion Questions for This Case

1. What might Mr. Lewis have done to co-opt the parents in this situation?
2. What might Mr. Lewis have done to win the rabbi's and the president's support?
3. Can "legal action" work both ways? Can the synagogue look to its own counsel for advice on this case?
4. Could the final confrontation have been avoided?

Relating to Parents and Students

Case 27 ▾ Parents as Sources of Stress

Even for an experienced administrator, managing relationships with parents is "the biggest source of stress." Stanley Kravitz has worked in Jewish education for twenty-five years, and his conclusion is that "there are many parents you just can't satisfy. Either they think you are demanding too much of their children, or you are not giving them enough attention. I find myself negotiating constantly with parents over class assignments, scheduling, or time in the resource room for an LD student."

Over time Mr. Kravitz' has placed most emphasis on establishing standards of attendance, promptness, and the completion of assignments, but, he says, he's

up against the fact that yuppie parents don't like to be told what to do with their children. One of the things we do when there's a problem with a child is send a note home, telling what the issue is, like not doing homework. The notes always come back signed, but many of the parent don't do anything about it except make excuses for their children.

I've come to realize that taking a firm line with parents isn't enough in itself. For many children this school, this education, has no relevance for them in their life outside of school. Everything we do here is just what they do while they're in school; it's not part of life. Some of them have big questions about why they are doing it at all, and it angers them that they have no control over it.

I've been tough about setting standards. I'm not backing away from that. But I'm trying something new by taking a more therapeutic orientation in dealing with families. I make it clear that I know there is a problem of being Jewish in America and I understand ambivalence. I try to convince them that religious training is a two-way street. They can't just turn children over to us a few hours a week; they must take ownership and responsibility. I can't tell yet what the results are, but increasingly I feel this is an important part of my job.

See pages 88–89 for General Questions for All Case Vignettes and for The Guiding Principles of Leadership Practices.

Additional Discussion Questions for This Case

1. To what extent might the use of the label *yuppie parents* prevent the administrator from solving problems with a particular group of parents?
2. How could the teaching staff become involved with the issue of the parents' lack of commitment to their children's religious education?
3. Is the administrator assuming too much responsibility for this issue?
4. What assumptions is Mr. Kravitz making about the educational process?

Relating to Parents and Students

Case 28 ▾ A Question of Child Abuse

Doris Berger is an experienced part-time synagogue educator in a congregation in an industrial city in the Northeast. In addition to her administrative duties, she tutors a few children every year. One day a ten-year-old child described circumstances at her home that sounded very much like child abuse, and she threatened to run away or commit suicide. Obviously the child was very upset, but Ms. Berger was not sure whether the abuse was real or the child was dramatizing the situation. In addition, the child refused to talk to anyone else about it, and she insisted that her parents would "kill her" if Ms. Berger revealed to them that she knew what went on at home or if she reported the situation to anyone.

Ms. Berger was able to find out enough about the family to confirm that it was a troubled one and that the father was litigious. Still, Ms. Berger knew she had no choice but to report the situation to the authorities.

See pages 88–89 for General Questions for All Case Vignettes and for The Guiding Principles of Leadership Practices.

Additional Discussion Questions for This Case

1. What do you need to know about school law regarding situations such as this? How can you learn it?

2. Whom could Ms. Berger have turned to for consultation and assistance?

Relating to Parents and Students

Case 29 ▼ The Commitment of Parents and Students

Molly Gross is the principal of a supplementary school in a suburban community where there are many educational and recreational activities for children and families. During her twelve-year tenure, Ms. Gross has watched commitment to religious school dwindle. Parents give the school limited support; they are not motivating or encouraging their children. Ms. Gross believes that even more than ever before, the religious school has become secondary in importance to other activities. This has been demonstrated by poor attendance and the failure of students to complete homework assignments.

The lack of commitment has affected the teachers' morale, and Ms. Gross has begun to see adverse changes in their classroom preparation and even in their attendance. She has called in parents of the children with the worst attendance records and has given them "long, stern talks," but the improvement in attendance was short-lived, and overall the situation has continued to deteriorate. Many solutions have been proposed, but Ms. Gross is afraid that overly restrictive policy changes, such as "no homework, no promotion," would simply drive families away altogether. "At least this way," she pointed out "we have them part of the time."

See pages 88–89 for General Questions for All Case Vignettes and for The Guiding Principles of Leadership Practices.

Additional Discussion Questions for This Case

1. Whom should Ms. Gross turn to for help?

2. Whose job is it to fix the problem?
3. How might a clearer statement of mission help the students?
4. To what extent is this situation different from that in a day school?

Relating to Other Professionals in One's Organization

Case 30 ▼ The Controlling Boss*

At the age of thirty, Eugene Gold became the educational director of a large Conservative congregation in the Midwest. There are more than four hundred children in the religious school, and Mr. Gold is responsible for supervising the educational program from nursery school through grade eight and participating in the governance of a community high school.

Mr. Gold faced a difficult beginning with the school board, in large part, he felt, because of the rabbi's presence at the meetings. The rabbi had been in the congregation for twenty-three years, and although he planned to retire within two years, he had not relinquished his strong control over all phases of the congregation's activities. His own candidate for the position of educational director, a man older than Mr. Gold, was a close friend of the rabbi's, and he made no secret of his disagreement with the choice of Mr. Gold. According to Mr. Gold,

> He made it a practice to second-guess every proposal and decision that I brought to the school board. He also created problems. For example, one spring, the rabbi suggested to the school board that there had been too many snow days [school cancellations] and that the United Synagogue policy on minimum number of school days had been violated. I suggested that to the best of my knowledge, the United Synagogue does not have such a policy.

---

* This vignette can also be used to illustrate the skill area of Managing Lay-Professional Relations.

Nonetheless, the board instructed Mr. Gold to devise a strategy for adding extra days to the calendar.

Whenever there was any difficulty with a professional staff member of the congregation, the rabbi and the president of the congregation met with the professional. One time Mr. Gold received a call from the president, inviting him to lunch. When he arrived, the rabbi was there also, and the lunch was staged as an occasion for bringing up some complaints about the school and Mr. Gold's handling of it.

See pages 88–89 for General Questions for All Case Vignettes and for The Guiding Principles of Leadership Practices.

Additional Discussion Questions for This Case

1. How could Mr. Gold play a more active role in structuring the supervisory conferences with the rabbi?
2. How might the educational director educate the laypersons about the situation?
3. Would a clearer job description help? How would it help? If it would not, why not?

Suggested Options

1. Mr. Gold should meet alone with the rabbi to ascertain the rabbi's understanding of the school and his needs and aspirations for it and to find areas of agreement. He can suggest that they meet regularly so that Mr. Gold can apprise the rabbi of developments in the school and the rabbi can offer his own expertise and advice as situations arise. Part of the discussion should involve the process of interacting with laypersons, so that when they disagree privately, they do not make the disagreement public.

2. Mr. Gold should meet alone with the president of the congregation to try to establish his own professional position and to ask for suggestions on how he might develop a better relationship with the rabbi during the time that remains and during the transition period. Mr. Gold may also request that the president speak to him alone should there be a perceived problem with his work, rather than placing him in the untenable position of being the subject of a team critique by the rabbi and the president.

3. Mr. Gold should develop a political alliance with the school board and the synagogue board, working constantly to maintain positive public relations in behalf of the school and himself. Concurrently he must work hard to strengthen the school board, ensuring a strong school and a strong director of education.

Relating to Other Professionals in One's Organization

Case 31 ▾ Transitions[*]

After five years as a part-time administrator for a small innovative community high school, Alice Kaufman became the principal of a medium-size school (about 220 students), K–12, in a suburban congregation. Her experience with the high school had been successful and gratifying, and she made the transition with confidence and with the support of her colleagues.

Ms. Kaufman began the job right after a tumultuous and divisive year in the congregation, during which there was a bitter split in sentiment among members and the rabbi was terminated. An interim rabbi was filling the role. In addition, the building was in serious disrepair, and janitorial service was almost nonexistent. Ms. Kaufman had come into a situation where the morale of both the staff and the parents was low, and she soon learned that neither wanted changes in the school. Despite what she thought was her mandate to pursue excellence in the school, Ms. Kaufman was forced to work in the shadow of her predecessors and among the remnants of what appeared to be a disorganized and casual leadership style. "I thought they wanted a maverick," she said, "but it turned out they wanted a groupie."

Ms. Kaufman is organized, full of plans, and outspoken. But her previous training did not prepare her to deal with parents who became confrontational over the scheduling of a bar or bat mitzvah ceremony, nor did it help her to combat the stresses of low morale and poor services, nor did it suggest a way to revitalize a

---

[*] This vignette can also be used to illustrate the skill area of Managing Oneself.

staff that apparently could not be motivated. Her first year was frustrating and painful; it was also lonely, for there was no rabbinic leadership, and there were no colleagues with whom she could discuss her problems (the congregation does not have any other full-time professionals on its staff).

Thus, Ms. Kaufman was eager to work with the new rabbi, whom the congregation had engaged and whom she had met during the interview process. She said,

> I looked forward to having him as a colleague. I was sure that he would want to be involved in the school. I was enthusiastic, and I took him into my confidence. I described my ambivalence about working with the bar mitzvah parents. I also discussed my reactions to the staff and described the attraction that the students had for the Chabad rabbi who occasionally taught in the school. His response to that was there were not enough people from our movement teaching in the school. In our many conversations during the early part of the school year, he often said to me, "You always speak with such authority." I took this as a compliment and only later reflected on what this really meant.

After a conversation with the rabbi in December of his first year, when Ms. Kaufman was again confiding in him about some problems in the school, the rabbi said he thought she should consider doing something else, that she should not stay on in the job after the school year. He said that because she was the focus of some complaints about the school, "I can't survive here if I have to worry about you and my job. I have to restore the dignity of the rabbinate, the adult education program, and good feelings in this congregation." Ms. Kaufman was left to serve as a lame duck principal for the remainder of the school year.

See pages 88–89 for General Questions for All Case Vignettes and for The Guiding Principles of Leadership Practices.

Additional Discussion Questions for This Case

1. To what extent can you attribute the principal's departure to the rabbi's lack of support? To what extent can you attribute it to her own naïveté?
2. How could Ms. Kaufman have gotten better information on the desires of parents and the staff?
3. What should one do in the first year as a principal, and what should one not attempt to do?
4. Was it time for Ms. Kaufman to move on?

Managing Day-to-Day Operations

Case 32 ▼ Coordinating or Competing?*

Leah Black feels fortunate to be directing a religious school in a community where the synagogue is seen as a major center of activity and where there is a great deal of participation in Jewish life. The synagogue building is large and has varied facilities and meeting rooms, and it is also extremely well used. Thus, an important annual event is the calendar meeting, for which Ms. Black joins with representatives of the board, the sisterhood, the men's club, the youth groups, the singles' groups, and the senior citizens' organization, as well as with other professionals in the synagogue to plan the year's schedule.

Ms. Black has learned that the only way she can secure the facilities she needs for the school's program is to come to the meeting with a completely prepared calendar. She knows the demands of the other groups which might come into conflict with her program. Since she became the director of the school four years ago, she has successfully scheduled holiday celebrations, staff-development sessions, parent-education programs, parent meetings, special services, and anything else she needed. This year, however, the senior citizens' program has almost doubled in size, and the congregation has extended the hours of its nursery school. The activities director and the nursery school director are adamant about their needs for the meeting rooms at the same time that Ms. Black is planning a major parent-education program. She says, "I

---

* This vignette can also be used to illustrate the skill areas of Relating to Other Professionals in One's Organization and Managing Space.

find it a great strain to deal with this. I don't want to create hard feelings, but I don't know how we are going to resolve this dilemma."

See pages 88–89 for General Questions for All Case Vignettes and for The Guiding Principles of Leadership Practices.

Additional Discussion Questions for This Case

1. To what extent was there a structure or a set of procedures by which to negotiate competing interests?
2. What effort was made to bring the issue to the attention of the rabbi and the director of the senior citizens' program.
3. Has Ms. Black overlooked some opportunities that can not only resolve the dilemma but also improve the school's program? If so, what are some of those opportunities?

Suggested Options

1. Ms. Black should meet with the rabbi, the president, and the executive director of the congregation to express her concerns. She might suggest that the synagogue's statement of mission be reviewed (or created) to determine where the congregation's priorities lie. Where possible, links between the various programs should be created. For example, the directors of the school, the nursery school, and the seniors' organization can develop intergenerational programs that benefit everyone. The staff could then meet with the board to establish policies on space allotment based on the statement of mission. They may also consider a planning retreat, which could also help each constituent group understand the needs of the other.
2. Efforts should be made to find space outside the synagogue for some activities. This could entail renting space or adding mobile units to the property.

3. Space-planning consultants could be brought in to assess how the available space might be used more efficiently. Larger spaces may be broken down into multipurpose areas by means of partitions. Some special-purpose spaces, such as the sanctuary or the larger offices, might be used for some meetings.

Managing Day-to-Day Operations

Case 33 ▼ Principal Support and Program Adaptation*

Sondra Arons, the director of the preschool, was asked to take over as principal of the religious school when the principal resigned in midyear. Her children were students in the school, and she had served on the school committee. She knew the school's problems, and was very committed to its success. She also needed the additional income. For all these reasons, she accepted the position.

One of the school's special programs was a pre–bar and bat mitzvah program conducted by Sue Klein, a staff member of the Jewish family service (JFS) organization. The program was a component of the Jewish Family Life Education (JFLE) program, which is sponsored by the JFS. It operates as a "pull out" program. That is, the group of students who would become bar or bat mitzvah during the upcoming eight months were excused from class for the half-hour workshops, which focus on the meaning of the bar or bat mitzvah ceremony and its relationship to issues of adolescence. For each series there was also one meeting at which the children in the program and their parents met with Ms. Klein.

The program was fairly successful, although Ms. Klein sometimes had problems controlling the behavior of the group. Twelve-year-olds are often the most disruptive students in religious school, and the students often saw the pull-out time as an opportunity to fool around. Their teacher was usually busy with the rest

---

* This vignette can also be used to illustrate the skill areas of Managing Change and Relating to Parents and Students.

of the class and could offer only minimal help. The parent component had unpredictable attendance from one year to another.

Mrs. Arons' predecessor had accepted the program but treated it as a service of JFLE; she did not see it as an integral part of the school curriculum and provided little assistance. Mrs. Arons, however, believed in the program; her own daughter had found it very meaningful two years earlier. She lent a great deal of support to the sessions that included the parents, by sending notices home and making phone calls to encourage the parents to attend. And attendance improved dramatically. In addition, a fortuitous circumstance changed the nature of the program. This year, all the students in the class were eligible at the same time. Mrs. Arons suggested that the class teacher, who was also the cantor and teacher of the bar and bat mitzvah students, co-teach the class with Ms. Klein. This setup not only helped with classroom management, but it also gave more time to the workshop and more meaning to its content.

See pages 88–89 for General Questions for All Case Vignettes and for The Guiding Principles of Leadership Practices.

Additional Discussion Questions for This Case

1. How can a principal help teachers work with students in difficult age groups?
2. What kinds of experiences are appropriate for twelve-year-olds?

Managing Day-to-Day Operations

Case 34 ▾ Management Skills for a Rural Camp*

According to two experienced administrators, there are multiple challenges to managing a kosher educational summer camp in a rural area. To be attentive to safety and kashrut in an area where the issues associated with kashrut are unfamiliar is a major management issue. One of the administrators explained,

> We needed to pre-plan carefully, pre-buy, and arrange for storage. We didn't have a sufficiently large refrigeration unit in camp, so to ensure kashrut and noncontamination, we had to build movable partitions in a public-storage refrigeration locker and have sole use of a truck.
>
> To meet our needs, eventually we bought a freezer and a generator. To do that, we had to know government regulations. Then we got into government commodities to hold down cost. But you have to pay storage and transportation on these—which include flour, butter, dried milk, rice, and beans. Since these are administered through state government, you also have all the complications of working through government bureaucracies. You have to learn to keep really detailed and accurate records.

In all areas it was important that decisions be made and actions taken not just on grounds of expediency but within the framework of the institution and with its goals in mind. There was a need to interpret policies to the staff, to vendors, and even to parents:

---

* This vignette can also be used to illustrate the skill areas of Adjusting Vision and Setting Goals, Managing Staff, and Managing Space.

For example, in the kitchen you have to hire a supervisor who sets the right educational tone, so supervisory staff get training in New York before camp begins. With vendors you have to balance good business practices and good ethical practices. You are dependent on good relationships with vendors in this totally non-Jewish environment. With parents you have to establish that there is no coming and going on Shabbat. You make the rules up front, and you have to know you have the backing up the line from the institution and the lay board.

Hiring and firing is a sensitive issue in terms of the ethical and moral dimensions of a Jewish institution. It's very important that people who are fired be able to leave quietly. It's our responsibility to make sure that transportation is arranged and they can get home. Camp management is a balancing act.

See pages 88–89 for General Questions for All Case Vignettes and for The Guiding Principles of Leadership Practices.

Additional Discussion Questions for This Case

1. In what ways not described in the case vignette is a Jewish educational camp different from a secular educational camp?

2. In what ways is directing a summer camp of this kind similar to directing a day school? In what ways is it similar to directing a supplementary school? What management skills overlap? What skills are transferable to and from this kind of educational setting?

Managing Oneself

Case 35 ▾ Transitions Are Never Easy*

One year after a new rabbi was hired, Faith Adler was hired to be the education coordinator of the Sunday portion of a supplementary school in an affluent suburb. The rabbi who had founded the synagogue and served during its first ten years of existence had recently died of cancer, and the congregation was still grieving. The rabbi who succeeded him—the rabbi who came to the congregation a year before Ms. Adler arrived—did not have a personality strong enough to overcome the his predecessor's reputation. After his first three years, his contract was not renewed.

This second period of transition was also a delicate one, and it presented several problems for Ms. Adler. She had been hired to revitalize the congregation's young families by revamping, professionalizing, and modernizing the religious school. This was her first job as an administrator, and in the two years that she had worked in this position, she felt she was close to achieving her goals, and she was very optimistic about the future. When a new rabbi was hired, Ms. Adler heard a rumor that he wanted her to vacate her position so that he could bring on someone of his choosing. She knew she was popular with the board and wondered whether she should approach the board members directly to "lobby" for her position. Or should she just let the new rabbi have his own team and go looking for another job?

See pages 88–89 for General Questions for All Case Vignettes and for The Guiding Principles of Leadership Practices.

---

* This vignette can also be used to illustrate the skill area of Managing Lay-Professional Relations.

Additional Discussion Questions for This Case

1. Should the education coordinator trust the grapevine?
2. How should she approach the new rabbi?
3. Should she consult with or lobby a strong supporter on the board? Why or why not?

Suggested Options

1. Ms. Adler should request a meeting with the rabbi to ascertain his needs, interests, and goals and to determine whether each of them feels that she can help him achieve his vision of the synagogue's mission. Such a meeting may result in a better understanding between the two of them, and it may help the rabbi to realize that Ms. Adler is capable and qualified to be his partner.

2. Ms. Adler may want to consult with the president of the board or with the chairperson of the school to discuss her feelings and ask for some suggestions on how to proceed. By no means should she begin to lobby board members for her job. That would alienate the rabbi and create a situation that would only weaken Ms. Adler's position.

3. Perhaps Ms. Adler could suggest a planning process whereby the rabbi, the board, and all constituencies would be involved in identifying the mission of the school and the synagogue in general. This course of action would depersonalize the issue, so that it would no longer be a question of a new rabbi who wants to replace a senior staff member with his own team.

Managing Oneself

Case 36 ▾ Forced Retirement*

A senior educator in his sixties was the director of education for the federation of Jewish agencies in a populous area. During his six-year tenure he introduced many new programs, all of which were successful in gaining community recognition and establishing momentum. He created in-service programs for educators and community workers, he organized several community-wide cultural events, and he had begun a program of adult Jewish education.

During his sixth year at the job, he was informed that the structure of the agency was being reorganized at the community level. At the recommendation of JESNA, a commission on Jewish education was being formed, and his position at the federation would be eliminated. With the endorsement of many rabbis, educators, and other professionals in the Jewish community, he applied for the new position but was passed over in favor of a younger educator from out of state.

From "a leak in the system," he learned that his application was rejected on the basis of his being "too close to retirement." The educator was deeply hurt and was angry at this evidence of age discrimination since he felt he was still alert, vigorous, and able to contribute to Jewish education and the community. He had no interest in retiring, and he wondered whether he had any recourse to "fight the decision" without embarrassment to himself or to the Jewish community.

See pages 88–89 for General Questions for All Case Vignettes and for The Guiding Principles of Leadership Practices.

---

* This vignette can also be used to illustrate the skill area of Managing Lay-Professional Relations.

Additional Discussion Questions for This Case

1. How can educators learn more about the ways in which labor laws affect schools?
2. Was this senior educator justified in his anger?

Managing Oneself

Case 37 ▼ Learning to Use Resources*

Nancy Rosen spent four years as a teacher and then as a part-time coordinator of a small religious school in a suburban Reform congregation. During that time she took courses in education and in Jewish studies at a nearby college and took part in some in-service programs that were offered by the bureau of Jewish education. When a larger religious school in another Reform synagogue in the area advertised for an educational director, she felt she had attained the confidence and skills that such a position required. She applied for the job and was pleased when it was offered to her.

Ms. Rosen felt she could handle the responsibilities that were described in her contract: supervising the religious school program from prekindergarten through high school, supervising as well as teaching in the midweek Hebrew school, which was attended by students in the fourth through seventh grades, and assisting with the adult- and parent-education programs. From a discussion with the school committee that took place during the interview process, she also knew that there was interest in revising the curriculum, something that had not been done for many years.

Ms. Rosen began the job with great enthusiasm. Based on her prior experience, she assumed she could rely on both the chairperson of the school committee and the rabbi for support and assistance. She decided she would spend the first year getting acquainted with the faculty, reviewing the curriculum, and slowly initiating changes.

---

* This vignette can also be used to illustrate the skill area of Managing Lay-Professional Relations.

Before very long, however, Ms. Rosen became totally overwhelmed. The curriculum was not only old but almost totally unused. Classes ranged from the highly structured to the highly playful, and there was an undercurrent of dissatisfaction with the school, among both teachers and parents. And the time she had for either observing and evaluating the work of the teachers or working with them directly was limited because most of them worked only part-time, on Sundays, and she herself had to teach part-time in the midweek Hebrew school. Furthermore, unlike the chairperson of the school committee in her previous school, who was very much involved in all operations of the school, the school committee chair in the new congregation had a busy professional practice and little time for the school. And although the rabbi was available to provide moral support, he did not take an aggressive interest in the school, nor was he able to commit much time to it.

Ms. Rosen felt totally isolated. Where should she begin? Should she assess the skills and interests of the faculty? Should she begin with a curriculum committee, and if so, how can she persuade part-time teachers to participate? How can she get help?

See pages 88–89 for General Questions for All Case Vignettes and for The Guiding Principles of Leadership Practices.

Additional Discussion Questions for This Case

1. How might this case have been different if Ms. Rosen had had more experience?
2. How could she restructure the job to handle it better?
3. Are there external resources available that she might take advantage of? If so, what are they?

Managing Oneself

Case 38 ▾ Part-Time Jobs Can Take Full-Time Management*

In hiring administrators, congregations may be forced by resource constraints to combine roles, creating a single full-time position. Knowing this, Florence Berkman came to her interview at a Conservative congregation in a small city determined not to be both educational director and teacher. "It's just a way for them to get another teacher on the cheap," she said. "I was convinced that I could not supervise teachers, do observations, and improve the quality of instruction if I spent half my time teaching in a classroom." Nonetheless, she did accept the full-time position, which was clearly part educational director (75 percent of the responsibilities) and part youth director (25 percent of the responsibilities), when it was explained that group leaders would work directly with the students, and her job as youth director would simply be "supervising the program."

Ms. Berkman described the experience:

> Soon I found out that I was spending a lot of time in the office supervising my two part-time jobs. There was no secretary; parents were in and out. In trying to get budget for more support services, I realized *I* was doing too much of the parents' work. I decided to see what I could change, to see if I could teach this place about boundaries. First I did what I could do independently. I put a sign on my

---

* This vignette can also be used to illustrate the skill areas of Defining Roles, Managing Lay-Professional Relations, and Relating to Parents and Students.

door that said, "I am observing the following classes at nine, ten, and one o'clock. My office hours are. . . ." When parents complained, I told them, "I am the conductor, not a member of the orchestra."

I was able to use the parents in the political process to bring my concerns before the board. I got them to raise the issue of support services, my need for a secretary, and maintenance issues. It was parents, not me, who told them that those things were keeping me from the work I should be doing. They created the support system for me, and I accepted the limitations that could not be changed. Things are working well now, and I feel in control of my time.

See pages 88–89 for General Questions for All Case Vignettes and for The Guiding Principles of Leadership Practices.

Additional Discussion Questions for This Case

1. Is combining two jobs to create a full-time position an appropriate option? Under what conditions can it work?
2. What other options could Ms. Berkman have employed to secure more support services?

Managing Oneself

Case 39 ▾ People Time versus Paper Time*

After eleven years as a teacher in a K–6 day school, Muriel Cushner was delighted when she was asked to be principal. Although she had been an active faculty member and a leader among the teachers, Ms. Cushner had no executive experience in a formal setting. At first she spent a great deal of time interacting with teachers in regard to a variety of educational and interpersonal issues. These were situations in which she felt most comfortable. Many people, however, felt that this was not an appropriate use of her time and were concerned that she was neglecting much administrative work. She remarked,

> I have been advised to be more careful with my time and to be strict about having people, especially teachers, make an appointment. But these teachers were my colleagues only last year. How can I treat them like I think I'm a big shot?
>
> When I am in the office, I face questions of a purely administrative nature. I do scheduling and ordering; I keep track of the calendar and do reports and other paperwork. And of course, I take phone calls from parents and board members and anybody else that wants to talk to me. I sit there doing these things, and I think about how I could be observing teachers or writing curricula or developing training sessions. I sometimes wonder, Why did they hire a teacher if my skills are going to be wasted sitting in the office?

---

* This vignette can also be used to illustrate the skill area of Defining Roles.

See pages 88–89 for General Questions for All Case Vignettes and for The Guiding Principles of Leadership Practices.

Additional Discussion Questions for This Case

1. To what extent is the principal having difficulty accepting the role of administrator?
2. What issues does a teacher confront in taking a promotion to supervise her former colleagues?
3. What are the advantages and disadvantages of promoting from within? What factors can facilitate the successful transition when someone is promoted from within?
4. Is Ms. Cushner wasting her skills or failing to acquire new ones?

Managing Oneself

Case 40 ▼ Stress for the Young Administrator*

During her early college days Natalie Bloom chose a career in Jewish education. She had been a student at an intensive Hebrew high school, studied at a Hebrew college at the same time she attended a regular university, and completed a master's in contemporary Jewish studies and education. By the age of twenty-five, after completing school and having taught part-time for seven years, she became the educational director of a suburban congregational school of 250 students. Like many of her colleagues, particularly those in congregations that are not resource rich and have a limited professional staff, Ms. Bloom discovered that she must answer to many demands. Among other responsibilities she served as director of adult education and the junior congregation, supervised the nursery school (although there was a nursery school director), taught in the community high school, and attended countless meetings at both the synagogue and the bureau of Jewish education.

She soon found that her many roles created stress and demands on her time that interfered with her ability to concentrate on her development as an educational leader. She also found that a particular source of stress as a young administrator was carrying out her role as a supervisor of teachers.

Even in a fairly large metropolitan area the field of Jewish education is a small world, and Ms. Bloom soon found herself supervising a former fellow student as well as many people much older than she, including her aunt. She described her predicament:

---

* This vignette can also be used to illustrate the skill area of Managing Staff.

I had a really hard time with the former fellow student, who was even more uncomfortable with the change in our relative status than I was. It was very awkward when I had to observe or evaluate her. Often when I stood outside of her class, I noticed that she had some problems with classroom management and discipline. But she was very defensive when I tried to make some suggestions as to how she might improve her approach in order to keep the attention of the students.

Given the advanced ages of some of the members of the staff, one question that was asked at Ms. Bloom's interview was whether she felt she would have any difficulty dealing with teachers who were closer to her mother's age than to her own. But she found it was sometimes easier to work with the older staff members:

One of the things I tried to do in the school was to introduce some new curriculum materials and instructional techniques. Even though the older people find it harder to change, we were able to talk about it. Even my aunt let me help her understand how to use some new curriculum and techniques we were trying in the school. Still, every so often when I would make a suggestion, a teacher would say to me, "I was teaching before you were in diapers." I tried not to pay attention to those remarks, but it was sometimes difficult. One situation that I found particularly hard to handle was with a veteran teacher who taught the *vav* class, the highest grade. It is very hard to get a teacher who is knowledgeable enough to teach that grade. She is competent, but I felt she could improve. However, she is extremely sensitive to criticism, and I often toned down my critique of her more than I really wanted to.

See pages 88–89 for General Questions for All Case Vignettes and for The Guiding Principles of Leadership Practices.

Additional Discussion Questions for This Case

1. Does Ms. Bloom appear to understand the process of conducting a performance review?
2. What are the important steps in providing constructive feedback?
3. Why might the youth or the seniority of subordinates have been so problematic for Ms. Bloom?

Managing Oneself

Case 41 ▼ Time for Oneself

Janet Taub is a competent and experienced educator. She is a
graduate of the Teachers Institute of the Jewish Theological
Seminary and highly values the teaching of biblical text. When
asked what a religious-school educational program should be, she
says she views herself as a "traditionalist," but she asserts that she
also appreciates the importance of "experiential education."

For the past eleven years she has been a full-time educational
director in a large suburban congregational school. She finds her
job satisfying but very demanding:

I arrive at my office by 10:00 A.M., and I am here until at
least 7:00 P.M. most evenings. And at least twice a month
there is an evening meeting. I am busy with parents, with
teachers, recruiting, reviewing lesson plans, textbooks,
meetings at the bureau, negotiating with the executive
director, keeping the rabbi informed, meeting with my
school committee chair, answering or returning phone
calls, ordering supplies—you name it. It never ends. Even
after eleven years in this school, which is pretty well organized and well run, I am constantly problem solving or
responding to crises. And of course, I have other responsibilities when I get home.

Mrs. Taub has one primary complaint:

I really believe in education, and I really believe in the
study of Torah, but I have a real problem: there is no time

for me to study—no time for *Torah Lishma,* "study for its own sake." Deep down I don't believe you can be a good Jewish educator unless you are a role model and continue to study and learn. So even though I feel I am a competent administrator, I sometimes think I am a failure as an educator.

See pages 88–89 for General Questions for All Case Vignettes and for The Guiding Principles of Leadership Practices.

Additional Discussion Questions for This Case

1. How realistic are Mrs. Taub's expectations about being a good educator?
2. Should she feel she is a competent administrator? Why or why not?

Managing Oneself

Case 42 ▼ Understand Traditions, Then Make Changes*

Ruth Silver was brought into the day school as coordinator of Judaic studies. The school didn't have a written curriculum for Judaic studies; Ms. Silver was expected to coordinate and document the curricula that teachers were using, supply texts and resources, and provide teachers with training and support. She described the experience:

I anticipated that I would get a lot of support from teachers. At the interview, I was told that there was a lot of teacher involvement at this school and that teachers all wrote their own curriculum at the beginning of the year. I was also told that teachers would welcome training. On the basis of my initial observations in classrooms, I realized some teachers needed a more extensive repertoire of teaching skills and that some needed a better understanding of the content they were dealing with.

At a staff meeting I shared my observations with the staff and said that I would work with them to write better curricula, get resources that help them, and bring in experts to provide training. You can't believe how hostile they were; all they heard was that I was criticizing. So I backed off and let the whole thing go for a while.

I still thought that there was teacher involvement at this school and that my mistake was being too "top

---

* This vignette can also be used to illustrate the skill area of Managing Change.

down." So at another meeting I had the idea that in terms of holiday programming, we should all work in a collaborative fashion. Teachers would each sign up for a holiday and be in charge of all the programming. There was tremendous resistance. All I heard was "extra responsibility," "burden," and lots of anger.

When I dug a little deeper into the traditions at that school, I learned that the curriculum coordinator, who had been a teacher, was doing all the work that was supposed to be teacher involvement. Teachers gave her ideas, and she wrote the curriculum for all of them. When we talked about it, she said that she felt it was important that you do a lot of work for teachers to show that they could depend on you. Her whole idea was not to put any burdens on teachers and to give them endless support—even when they weren't doing a good job.

See pages 88–89 for General Questions for All Case Vignettes and for The Guiding Principles of Leadership Practices.

Additional Discussion Questions for This Case

1. What was the principal error Ms. Silver committed when she first came to the school?
2. What are some lessons from the literature on educational change that would have been helpful to Ms. Silver?
3. What strategies can be used to encourage teachers to use the resources and assistance available to them?

Managing Space

Case 43 ▼ An Issue of Sharing Space*

A big Reform congregation in a suburban community had long ago built a large wing to accommodate its religious school. Most of the religious school classes took place on Shabbat and Sunday mornings, but students were required to attend Hebrew classes two afternoons a week in preparation for their bar or bat mitzvah. In addition, the two-year confirmation program took place midweek, late in the afternoon. Thus for a few hours the space was very well used.

Still, the building was largely underutilized, not only for several days a week, but for most of the hours during the day. Many congregants were uncomfortable with so much quality space going largely unused, especially since it was expensive to maintain.

This issue was addressed to some degree several years ago, when there was an expressed need for more nursery schools in the community. The board of trustees had decided to meet this need by establishing a nursery school and hiring a director to run it. The nursery school was set up as a completely separate entity from the religious school. In fact, synagogue membership was not a requirement for enrollment in the nursery school, though it was for enrollment in the religious school. On the contrary, the nursery school enrollment policy was considered to be a potential marketing strategy, an opportunity for young families to become familiar with the synagogue and its programs. The nursery school was very popular with some of the leaders on the board, especially when it also turned out to be a profit maker for the synagogue.

---

* This vignette can also be used to illustrate the skill area of Relating to Other Professionals in One's Organization.

From the beginning, however, the nursery school was a major source of stress for the educational director and the chair of the school board. The nursery school was sharing space with the religious school, using the same rooms in the morning that the religious school used several afternoons a week. The educational director had several clashes with the nursery school director about how the rooms should be arranged on the days that the religious school classes met, where things should be stored, and other issues of control over the space. Some parents of the religious school students were disturbed that they were losing control over the school wing to people who were not synagogue members. The school board chair and the educational director also had many discussions over the impact of the nursery school on recruitment of students to the mid-week Hebrew classes. The director said, "It's hard enough to get kids of this age to attend religious school. When they see the childlike nature of the rooms, it turns them off even more."

See pages 88–89 for General Questions for All Case Vignettes and for The Guiding Principles of Leadership Practices.

Additional Discussion Questions for This Case

1. Are the educational director and the school board chair justified in their concern about sharing space with the nursery school?
2. What practices or policies would help keep the peace?

Suggested Options

1. The educational director should request that the president of the congregation call a meeting of the two directors and their

board chairs to try to come up with the best possible compromises. Prior to the meeting each director should solicit suggestions from the teachers. After coming up with a system of sharing, both directors must take responsibility for speaking to the teachers involved to elicit their support.

2. The educational director should elicit the congregation's support for the investment of some of the nursery school–generated income in improving the planning and design of the space. The plan should include innovative storage for materials and furniture and movable partitions behind which the nursery school's materials can be stored when the older children are using the space. The plan should also involve the maintenance staff, since they will be required to rearrange furniture and materials on a regular, almost daily basis. Teachers should be asked to determine what structures and arrangements will meet their needs and to make diagrams to help the maintenance staff rearrange the rooms accordingly.

3. The educational director should request that the president of the congregation call a meeting of the religious school committee and the parents of students in the religious school to address the issue of their resentment of the nursery school families. An increase in information and communication may diffuse the concerns of the religious school parents by demonstrating, for example, that the economic bonus of the nursery school is keeping religious school tuition lower and that the nursery school is attracting new members to the synagogue.

Managing Space

Case 44 ▼ Finding Space*

Herb Poston was the educational director of a supplementary school in a growing southeastern city. As the school began to outgrow the building in which it was housed, Mr. Poston approached the synagogue board to ask for help in finding a solution. The board was determined not to build an addition or buy a new building and asked Mr. Poston to come up with some alternative solutions. The board members offered some solutions of their own, which included making changes in the schedule (for example, instituting split sessions), renting satellite space or portable classrooms, and limiting enrollment.

At first Mr. Poston was hurt and disappointed by the board's refusal to consider building an addition to the school building, and he was distressed by the some of its recommendations, which he believed were detrimental to education. Rather than take a stand on the suggestions, however, he decided to seek input from others. He invited members of the education committee and architects from the congregation to define the options clearly and document the ways in which the board's suggestions would negatively affect the quality of education. Then the group surveyed the entire congregation in order to determine which direction to follow. They found support for minor scheduling changes, no support for portable classrooms, and a negative reaction to limiting enrollment in any way. The group finally decided to use partitions within the existing building in an attempt to use the space creatively, but Mr. Poston wasn't sure how long that solution would work.

---

* This vignette can also be used to illustrate the skill area of Managing Lay-Professional Relations.

See pages 88–89 for General Questions for All Case Vignettes and for The Guiding Principles of Leadership Practices.

Additional Discussion Questions for This Case

1. What do you think would have been a better strategy for getting the synagogue's leaders and experts to find solutions to the problem of limited space?
2. What are some of the creative uses of space that are available to Mr. Poston?

Managing Funds

Case 45 ▾ Money Is Power*

Alan Rosenberg was the educational director of the religious school of a large Conservative synagogue in a suburban community. He had ten years of administrative experience, and this was his second position in a well-established congregational school. He was extremely well organized and resourceful: his administrative skills were strong, and he prided himself on his time-management skills. His skillfulness was especially evident in the way he carefully prepared the budget plans and materials prior to the process of negotiating the school's budget.

The synagogue had a tradition of strong lay leadership and lay control over the organization's operations, and its well-defined budget process had been in place for many years. Each year the budget committee met with each professional staff member (for example, the educational director and the youth director) and with each committee chair to review budget plans and to talk about the needs of each department and the budget process itself. The lay leaders carried out the major negotiations and asked the professionals to defend their department's needs and account for the management of their area of responsibility.

Mr. Rosenberg took much more control of the budget process than his predecessors had—he came into the meetings with a carefully worked out budget plan. As the years went by, the members of the budget committee began to feel that their role was being threatened. They began to suspect that Mr. Rosenberg was using the budget process as a vehicle to control the relationship

---

* This vignette can also be used to illustrate the skill area of Managing Lay-Professional Relations.

between the lay leaders and the professionals. Although this situation did not result in a loss of funding for the school, it eventually contributed to tensions between Mr. Rosenberg and the board and led to the nonrenewal of his contract.

See pages 88–89 for General Questions for All Case Vignettes and for The Guiding Principles of Leadership Practices.

Additional Discussion Questions for This Case

1. What is the appropriate role of the educational director in the planning and budgeting processes?
2. What could Mr. Rosenberg have done to avoid the confrontation that he ultimately faced? What political skills did he ignore?

Suggested Options

1. Mr. Rosenberg would have benefited from a system in which he received ongoing feedback from his school board about how he was perceived. Perhaps an annual evaluation would have prevented his downfall. He might have solicited suggestions from other professionals or laypersons in the synagogue as well.
2. Mr. Rosenberg could have entered into more discussions with the chair and the board members about the role of the professional vis-à-vis the lay board. They might have talked about a variety of issues, including the budget-development process. Perhaps Mr. Rosenberg could have worked with some key individuals from the budget committee or the school board to develop the budget, thereby diffusing the issue of control and facilitating more lay ownership of the process.

3. Mr. Rosenberg could have shared his experiences and feelings with a colleague in the field on a regular basis. Sometimes an empathic outsider in a similar position can see aspects of a situation that the insider is unaware of.

Managing Funds

Case 46 ▼ Dealing with Budget Needs*

No matter how good a congregational school is and how good its reputation, obtaining adequate funds and resources can be a struggle for the administrator. Carol Weinstein, the full-time educational director in an affluent congregation in a large city, found this to be one of the most frustrating aspects of her job.

She explained that the difficulty in her congregation lies in the way the committees are structured and in the kinds of people that tend to serve on committees:

> In this congregation there is the temple board, the budget committee of the temple, and the school board. In many ways the three are unrelated. The budget committee is appointed by the president, and its members change almost every year—maybe because it is a thankless job. Also the budget committee has no real relationship to the school. A real problem is that the school board members are mostly younger parents or older intellectuals and have no real "power base" within the congregation. Since the school enjoys a good reputation, the budget committee is hesitant to increase the budget or add money for new programs. You know—if it's not broken, why fix it? The problem is if we continue this way, it will get broken. We have to figure out a way to convince the powers that be that we need a higher budget.

---

* This vignette can also be used to illustrate the skill area of Managing Lay-Professional Relations.

See pages 88–89 for General Questions for All Case Vignettes and for The Guiding Principles of Leadership Practices.

Additional Discussion Questions for This Case

1. If the educational director were to develop a plan to influence the powers that be, what should it consist of?
2. Who are the key actors to implement the plan?
3. How should the staff be involved?

Managing Funds

Case 47 ▾ A Dilemma in Fund-Raising

A new young executive director, Karen Dubin, was hired by the bureau of Jewish education in a midsize midwestern city with a cohesive and committed Jewish community. Most of the community can be characterized as middle class, although it has a limited number of wealthy Jewish families.

Toward the end of her first year in the job, Ms. Dubin embarked on a new project: raising money to subsidize youth programs in Israel. Her strong commitment to the project was based on her belief that six weeks in Israel can do more for a young person's Jewish identity and education than several years of supplementary school. After she had solicited funds from several individuals in the community, the executive board members of the bureau began to hear complaints that Ms. Dubin's fund-raising activities were taking money away from a major fund-raising priority in the Jewish community—Operation Exodus.

The board members felt they must curtail the young director's fund-raising but hesitated to diminish her enthusiasm and zeal for her job, which she was doing very well. Also, they basically agreed with her objective but feared alienating the community members who were committed to raising money for Operation Exodus or those who felt they were being asked support too many causes.

See pages 88–89 for General Questions for All Case Vignettes and for The Guiding Principles of Leadership Practices.

Additional Discussion Questions for This Case

1. In what ways might this case have been different in a larger

community? In what ways might it have been different in a smaller community?

2. What effect did Ms. Dubin's youth have on this process? What might have transpired if she had been older and more experienced?

3. Under what authority did she embark on the fund-raising campaign?

4. To what extent could she have made a stronger case for her campaign?

Managing Funds

Case 48 ▼ Budget Dilemma: A Conflict of Values*

Aviva Cantor is the principal of a large and well-established day school in the suburbs of a major city. The school has a very good reputation in the community and is considered to have a highly qualified teaching staff that has pioneered many innovative programs in both Judaic studies and general studies. The principal, faculty members, and school board also take pride in the school's success in placing a high value on academic excellence while maintaining a caring environment for its students.

In recent years Ms. Cantor has had to face a number of new challenges in her role as administrator. Whereas the school had built its reputation with a fairly homogeneous population, now the diversity of the student body has become an issue. The student population continues to be predominantly middle class, but a growing number of students have special needs, and so the demands for special services have grown. Some students are genuinely gifted, many are good students, others are average, and a growing number are learning disabled, emotionally troubled, or have limited English proficiency.

Ms. Cantor thinks that the diversity is in part a result of the school's reputation as a place that is receptive to all types of students. But she also believes that the demands and stresses on many families have changed in recent years, and she recognizes that, as in society at large, the school currently has more dual-career families, single-parent families, dysfunctional families, and

---

* This vignette can also be used to illustrate the skill area of Adjusting Vision and Setting Goals.

immigrant families than ever before. As a result, Ms. Cantor and the board are facing demands from all sides: requests for resource teachers for special needs, additional counseling services, tutoring programs, and challenging programs and equipment for the gifted.

Recently a couple with three children in the school came to Ms. Cantor. They were very distressed. Their two older children were successful students who coped well with the school and its dual curriculum, but the third child, now in the second grade, was clearly a problem. They were dedicated to the school and wanted a day school education for the child, and they urgently requested that the school provide a special class with more personalized attention. But the budget can be stretched only so far! If the school were to expend its resources in such a way, it would have to increase the size of its regular classes or jeopardize the gifted program. Could they make that decision? Could they refuse an intensive Jewish education for a child whose family desired it?

See pages 88–89 for General Questions for All Case Vignettes and for The Guiding Principles of Leadership Practices.

Additional Discussion Questions for This Case

1. What is the obligation of the Jewish day school to meet the needs of all potential students? Is it more like a public school for a specific population than a selective private school?
2. How should Ms. Cantor make the decision about resource trade-offs? Who else should be involved in the decision?

Managing Funds

Case 49 ▾ A Conflict of Interest in Funding

The bureau of Jewish education (BJE) in this midwestern city was very dependent on the federation of Jewish agencies for its support. The director was also dependent on the bureau's board members to advocate on the bureau's behalf during the annual proposal review and debate by the federation's allocations committee. In this city the agency directors normally made the presentations to the allocations committee but expected the laypersons to conduct the deliberations and influence the outcome.

Harriet Shaye, the director of the BJE, was particularly frustrated because she did not feel her agency had the support it needed from its lay board members. This lack of support was partly a reflection of the nature of volunteerism and partly a reflection of the organization's status in the local community. Many people served on several different boards and committees, and very few gave the BJE their primary loyalty. When Ms. Shaye made a presentation to the federation allocations committee, she was facing several committee members who were also on her agency's board. In this instance their primary loyalty was to the federation, and they aggressively questioned the budget requests. Ms. Shaye did not know how to handle this situation and muster the support that she and her agency needed.

See pages 88–89 for General Questions for All Case Vignettes and for The Guiding Principles of Leadership Practices.

Additional Discussion Questions for This Case

1. How could Ms. Shaye have prevented the situation that she faced when presenting her requests to the allocations committee?
2. What could she do to place less reliance on this type of funding process?

Managing Funds

Case 50 ▼ Converting Problems to Advantages*

Sometimes changes that appear to be potential catastrophes turn out to be positive events. Dr. Arnold Abramowitz, dean of a Hebrew college, found this to be so when his institution lost much of its funding from a federation of Jewish agencies. During the time that the college received 85 percent of its funding from the federation, it reflected a traditional conservatism, and any changes in the use of the funds were highly controlled and monitored by a federation committee. Within five years, however, revenue from the federation was reduced to 35 percent of the college's budgetary needs. Dr. Abramowitz found that after the institution had absorbed the shock, it was liberated in the kinds of things it could do with alternative sources of funding, both programmatically and administratively.

This was particularly evident when the college was forced to reduce its size due to the recession, a saturation of the adult education market, and the reduced federation allocation. The crisis was a particularly difficult challenge for Dr. Abramowitz because the college had many valuable assets, including a large and well-equipped facility, an experienced and diverse faculty and staff, a well-stocked and professionally staffed library and resource center, an established reputation, and accreditation. Dr. Abramowitz decided he must find a way to market these resources to those who needed them. In anticipation of a time when demand would once

---

* This vignette can also be used to illustrate the skill area of Managing Change.

again increase, he was determined to preserve the integrity and the capacities of the institution.

See pages 88–89 for General Questions for All Case Vignettes and for The Guiding Principles of Leadership Principles.

Additional Discussion Questions for This Case

1. Are there marketing opportunities that other educational institutions—such as Jewish community centers, synagogue schools, day schools, and bureaus of Jewish education—can use as an alternative to downsizing?

2. What effect might entrepreneurial activity have on the basic mission and goals of the institution?

Managing Funds

Case 51 ▼ The Pros and Cons of Merging*

Over a period of thirty years, a Solomon Schechter school in an East Coast city overcame its early problems of survival and eventually became a full K–8 school with its own facilities and support services, multiple classes in each grade, and a differentiated administrative staff. The school was ranked on a level with other independent schools in the region.

During the 1980s many young Jewish families moved to more remote suburbs of the city. Among these families were many who desired day school education for their children but were not willing to have them travel the substantial distance to the Schechter school. They also felt that the Schecter school had become too big, too bureaucratic, and too impersonal. They wanted to create a more intimate atmosphere. Soon a group of families felt it had the critical mass needed to start a school in their own community. They began the school with kindergarten and first grade. Because the school was so small and the resources so limited, they designated one of the teachers, Lila Shatz, as head teacher and school administrator. Ms. Shatz was to run the school in cooperation with the chair of the school board.

After a few years, when the initial excitement of creating a new school had faded, Ms. Shatz and the committee began to struggle with the realities of managing a school with few families and limited resources. They had to rent space and hire staff, but they could not afford the services of specialists. They also could not afford to lose the commitment of their clientele, although

---

* This vignette can also be used to illustrate the skill area of Managing Lay-Professional Relations.

some of the children had needs the the existing staff was not equipped to cope with.

Ms. Shatz, along with her counterpart in another small suburban day school, periodically consulted with the administrators of the large established school and with the bureau of Jewish education. Every now and then the laypersons and professionals would discuss the possibility of creating a formal link with the established school, but no one was fully comfortable with the idea, nor were they in agreement about the type of formal arrangements that they might establish. The trade-offs were not clear, but the leaders of the small school were reaching a point where they had to make some important decisions about how to run the school on a firmer financial and educational foundation.

See pages 88–89 for General Questions for All Case Vignettes and for The Guiding Principles of Leadership Practices.

Additional Discussion Questions for This Case

1. What are the trade-offs between a big institution and a small one?
2. How can schools take advantage of the resources available from a merger without losing their organizational and cultural ethos?
3. How might the small school creatively provide the services it needs and still retain its independence?

Managing Funds

Case 52 ▾ Seeking New Sources of Funding*

The bureau of Jewish education (BJE) in this West Coast city had been actively developing services and programs to meet the needs of a growing Jewish population. Saul Silverman, the executive director, had introduced a number of innovations in Jewish education since he assumed the post five years earlier, following several years as administrator of a Jewish summer camp. He was very pleased with his success in blending his experiences in informal and formal Jewish education and in managing a diverse staff. Directing a bureau provided him with an opportunity to utilize his skills in interpersonal and interorganizational management in a community that was ripe for development.

Nonetheless, Mr. Silverman was very frustrated with the limitations of the agency's resource base. Historically the bureau had functioned primarily on its allocation from the local federation of Jewish agencies. Unfortunately, the federation's allocation was dwindling at a time when the agency's potential services were expanding. Under Mr. Silverman's leadership the agency had been successful at creating a market for its services, at least in terms of client receptivity, although the client organizations were not typically able to pay much, if anything, for the services.

A similar frustration was felt by other federation-funded organizations, including those that were receptive to BJE services, such as the day school, the Jewish family service, and the community

---

* This vignette can also be used to ilustrate the skill areas of Managing Change and Managing Staff.

Hebrew high school. The executives in the field of Jewish education were becoming increasingly aware that they had to find alternative sources of funding, but none of them had experience in applying for funds or grants from foundations or in soliciting endowments. Mr. Silverman realized he could make a major contribution to Jewish education if he could tackle this problem. He needed to come up with a plan.

See pages 88–89 for General Questions for All Case Vignettes and for The Guiding Principles of Leadership Practices.

Additional Discussion Questions for This Case

1. What could the different organizations do cooperatively to maximize their resources and their ability to acquire new resources?

2. Where could the executives of these organizations turn to get information about the funding world and learn strategies for gaining access to funds? Who could help them?

Managing Funds

Case 53 ▼ Budgeting Assumptions: A Problem of Predictability[*]

Planning and budgeting for a Hebrew college must be done many months before the start of the institution's fiscal year. Many variables must be taken into account, including enrollment and tuition projections and anticipated allocations from a federation of Jewish agencies and other sources of revenue. Dr. Isaac Goldberg, the president of the college, successfully oversaw the process for several years with the help of the institution's business manager. Utilizing past experiences and data, they analyzed the college's four primary departments: the college, the graduate school, the high school, and the department of continuing education. The last three departments were growing significantly, with new programs in the graduate school, a new branch of the high school, and extensive marketing of the continuing education program. With its high volume and the relatively low cost of its instructional staff (all of whom worked part time and were hired on a contingency basis), the continuing education program had become an important source of revenue. After several successful years the budget was planned on the basis of a set of assumptions, including that the growth trajectory would continue, although at a slightly reduced rate (in order to estimate conservatively).

Two months into the academic year Dr. Goldberg was faced with a dilemma: enrollment did not match the budget assumptions, particularly in registration for the continuing education program, and the college was faced with a 20 percent shortfall in revenue. Major action had to be taken for both the short term and the long term. But how should the decisions be made? And what might be the implications of the decisions?

See pages 88–89 for General Questions for All Case Vignettes and for The Guiding Principles of Leadership Practices.

Additional Discussion Questions for This Case

1. Who should be involved in making decisions about midcourse corrections during a program year? What should the decision-making process entail?
2. What can administrators do to maintain the support of the staff when it is necessary to cut budgets and lay off some members of the staff?
3. Are there ways in which the administrators can increase the predictability of revenue sources in order to avoid serious surprises?

Managing Funds

Case 54 ▼ Difficult Decisions in Staff Development*

As the director of a day school, Dr. Elliot Katz felt he had a great deal of autonomy in allocating the school budget. He also had an excellent working relationship with the school board, and although the school had a financial manager, he was very much involved in planning the budget and was able to maintain control over a fund for special programs. A strong believer in staff development, he creatively found sources of funding to support the teachers who wanted to attend conferences and workshops. His staff was well aware of his passion for professional development and came to him often with requests for assistance in response to opportunities in that area.

Sometimes Dr. Katz had trouble deciding how to allocate the staff development dollars among competing priorities. Recently he had initiated a curriculum reform project. After much discussion with the Judaic studies staff, it was determined that the Bible and Midrash curriculum needed to be reworked in a more integrated fashion. There were few resources available, and Dr. Katz agreed to provide stipends for a group of teachers to develop the curriculum, purchase materials, and even consult with experts. He was particularly pleased because the Judaic studies faculty had in the past been more passive about staff development than had their counterparts in general studies.

After this decision was made, two general studies teachers came to Dr. Katz with a request for financial support to attend a workshop on the new national mathematics standards. The director was in a quandary: he knew the math workshop would be valuable, but, having committed funds to the Judaic studies project, he did not feel he could allocate funds to meet this new request. He had to work through the issue with the teachers without appearing to show favoritism.

See pages 88–89 for General Questions for All Case Vignettes and for The Guiding Principles of Leadership Practices.

Additional Discussion Questions for This Case

1. What can Dr. Katz do to facilitate staff participation without dipping into his shrinking funding pool? What other funding sources might he suggest?
2. In what ways is the curriculum project also a staff development project?
3. How might Dr. Katz change the process by which staff development funds are allocated?

Index

A

B

C

D

E

F

G

K

M

L

T

Teacher dismissal, 93–96, 137–38, 139–40

Teacher promotion, 121–22

Teacher recruitment, 143–44

Teacher supervision, 34–39, 134–36, 145–46, 184–86; clinical–supervision approach, 136

Team teaching, 116

Theft, 97–98

U

Unger, Arlyne, 79

W

Wachs, Saul, 79

Wexner Foundation, ix